WAITING FOR THE RAIN

Waiting
for the
Rain

An Iraqi Memoir

LAMEES AL ETHARI

MAWENZI
HOUSE

We acknowledge the support of the Canada Council for the Arts for our publishing program. We also acknowledge support from the Government of Ontario through the Ontario Arts Council.

Cover design by Sabrina Pignataro

Illustrations on pages ix, 3, 4, 8, 19, 28, 40, 41, 65, 141, 157 by Author.

A version of "The Zahawi Café", "Zahawi" was published in the *Malpais Review* (Vol. 2 No.2 Autumn 2011).

"Smoke" was published in "Poems of a Fallen City: Four Poems," *The New Quarterly*, no. 147, Fall 2018; and in *From the Wounded Banks of the Tigris*. London: Baseline Press, 2018.

Library and Archives Canada Cataloguing in Publication

Title: Waiting for the rain : an Iraqi memoir / Lamees Al Ethari.
Names: Ethari, Lamees Al, 1976- author.

Identifiers: Canadiana (print) 20190169753 | Canadiana (ebook) 20190169826 | ISBN 9781988449906 (softcover) | ISBN 9781988449913 (HTML) | ISBN 9781988449920 (PDF)

Subjects: LCSH: Ethari, Lamees Al, 1976- | LCSH: Ethari, Lamees Al, 1976-—Childhood and youth. | LCSH: Ethari, Lamees Al, 1976-—Family. | LCSH: Iraqis—Canada—Biography. | LCSH: Immigrants—Canada—Biography. | LCSH: Iraq—History—20th century. | LCSH: Iraq—History—21st century. | LCSH: Iraq—Social conditions—20th century. | LCSH: Iraq—Social conditions—21st century. | CSH: Iraqi Canadians—Biography.

Classification: LCC DS79.66.E84 A3 2019 | DDC 956.7044092—dc23

Printed and bound in Canada by Coach House Printing

Mawenzi House Publishers Ltd.
39 Woburn Avenue (B)
Toronto, Ontario M5M 1K5
Canada
www.mawenzihouse.com

For
Esam, Ameen and Hamza

خلاني وكتي وياك ريشة بوسط ريح
لا تثبت على الكاع و لا تقبل اتطيح

" عيني عيني "
سعدون جابر

My time with you has left me
like a feather in the wind:
unable to settle on land,
resisting descent.

    Sa'doun Jaber " 'Ani 'Ani"

In April 2006 I left Iraq.

In the three years after the American invasion, the beautiful country I had known was almost erased by incomprehensible violence and moral decay. We had become targets for the American troops and the countless factions of militias and gangs that began to plague our emptying neighborhoods. We had anticipated the loss and the destruction, but not the depth of chaos that would take over our streets.

I carry Iraq with me in memories that are braided together like the threads of the intricately designed woolen rugs that decorated our rooms and hallways. They are inserted in almost every one of my conversations and in the corners of all my notes: a story here, a doodle of palm trees there, and a hasty line or two from the old Iraqi songs my parents would serenade each other with on long summer road trips to the foothills of Sinjar.

Kitchener, Ontario

ONE

———

I was born in Iraq in the city of Kufa, but my father's family is originally from a very small village nearby, called Al-Harmia.

My father is the son of a clan-leader and landowner in southern Iraq who was well known and respected throughout the region for his generosity and discernment. According to my father, his family left the Arabian Peninsula over three hundred years ago and settled on a stretch of land alongside a distributary of the Euphrates called Chehat. I am not sure exactly where they migrated from at that time, but I have been told that the family lineage originated in Mecca some 1400 years ago, which is approximately the time when Prophet Muhammad lived there. The family name in Arabic, Al Ethari (or Al Athari), supposedly means "cultivator of land." They grow a short-grained, fragrant type of rice called "ambar," which is only found in southern Iraq.

Once, while looking at some old digitized maps saved on a CD, my father and I found an old British map of Iraq that identified our village by my great-grandfather's name. His house still stands, a short walk away from my grandfather's home. The older house, now abandoned, is what we call an eastern house (sharki)—it has a large courtyard open to the sky, surrounded by nine rooms that were the living quarters. It was perhaps built during the second half of the nineteenth century. There was a large hole in one of the outer walls, which was said to have been made by a British airplane during the 1920 Great Iraqi Revolution against the British Mandate. They say that my great-grandfather shot down the plane with a rifle, but it managed to drop a bomb on the house before it crashed. The house had become a local shrine, where people brought offerings of candles, henna, and sheep to be sacrificed. The oak doors were stained with handprints of henna and sheep's blood. A broken-down winding staircase led to a single room upstairs, which I managed to climb, rather awkwardly, my abaya wrapped around me. Unlike the other rooms in the rest of the house, it was well kept, neat, and freshly painted a very bright white with maroon trimmings where the walls met the ceiling. On the floor was a rug, and the room was stocked with Qurans as if the old patriarch still prayed and worshipped there. He had passed away when my grandfather was just fourteen.

Al-Harmia

Al-Harmia is one of my favorite places on earth. When you journeyed from Baghdad to Al-Harmia, the towns and cities in between gradually melted away into the earth, leaving a few homesteads scattered in a countryside of rice and wheat fields, date palms, reeds, and scrubby growth. The sparkling waters of the Euphrates rose to meet the road by Al-Kifl and it was as though time had stood still here while the rest of the world went on its way.

As we approached closer to my grandfather's home, we would come upon a site of traditional brickkilns, smoke billowing from their chimneys, hand-made bricks laid out in rows outside by the road to dry in the blistering sun. Fishermen in their mashoofs (canoes) would be waiting patiently for the small river fish to wander into their nets, and water buffalo bathed idly close to the banks of the distributaries. In the distance, I would glimpse women in black abayas collecting salt, the hems of their dresses and abayas stained a crusty white.

My grandfather's house rises like a small brick fortress in the middle of the rice fields, which are bright green and soft when the rice is young, and golden close to harvest time. The Chehat River bends its course here and flows close by. The house was built in the early 1940s; it had high, long and narrow windows and heavy oak double doors; there was a brass knocker in front. The brickwork around the entrance had been laid in a herringbone pattern, which had become indistinct with weather and age. Inside, the ceilings were high, and the windows let in slivers of sunlight. The entrance opened into the large living room, painted a light blue, with rooms on three sides. The house was cool in the summer; in the winter it was cold and each room was equipped with a kerosene heater, toward which we gravitated at night as the temperature dropped.

My father is the youngest of seven siblings: he has three sisters and three brothers. One of his older brothers, Ammo[1] Shakir, his family, and my youngest aunt, Amma Bassima, stayed on in my grandfather's house to care for my grandparents and oversee the land. My other aunts and uncles lived in neighboring towns and in Baghdad. The entire family would gather in the house during Eid al-Fitr and Eid al-Adha, all of us crowded inside the large living room. The adults never seemed to mind the chaos caused by so many children running about, unless it was time for their afternoon naps. We would be waved away into one of the rooms or told to go out to play in the garden, which had a large Nabug tree in the center and date palms all around the perimeter.

According to Amma Amel, in the past, the garden had been a fruit orchard surrounding the house. She would tell us that it used to be guarded by a large, black snake (erbeed). I never saw the snake, if

---

1   Ammo and Amma refer to the paternal uncle and aunt respectively. Usually, the terms are also used to address older men and women, and in-laws.

the story was true and it existed, because by the time I was born the orchard had perished due to a drought.

On late summer nights, I would sit on the rooftop with my family under white tentlike mosquito nets. Leaning back on our pillows we would count the stars and talk about times past and narrate traditions and stories from the Quran, and whisper rumors about djinns and giants stalking the villages. The scariest of all were the stories of Tantal, a folktale trickster. Every time I heard a sound or movement in the dark, I would imagine a tall and gangly creature with long arms, his footsteps striking the ground heavily as he roamed the fields around the house.

During the winter nights, Amma Bassima would cover us with heavy cotton-filled, hand-sewn quilts to keep us warm. We would fall asleep still talking and laughing, unwilling to waste a moment. Near dawn, I would wake up to the howl of dogs or the chimes of the grandfather clock in the hallway, and stir closer to my cousins and fall back asleep till the roosters woke me up an hour later.

Mornings brought the smell of date palm petioles and wood burning in the mud tanoors outside, as the women prepared them for baking the khubuz (flat bread). Soon the smell of the bread and the fragrance of the rice fields filled the air. The sounds of the busy household would force us to come out from under the heavy bedcovers and venture outside. Amma Bassima would be sitting with a smile next to the kerosene heater and a pot of steeped black tea laced with cardamom. A small istakan—a gold-rimmed glass on a saucer—would be neatly placed beside a pot of rice pudding bathed in churned butter sent from one of the neighboring houses.

Not far from the house was the Mudeef, a long one-room building that was the formal area for men's gatherings; it was usually where they welcomed male guests with lavish spreads of rice, slow-cooked lamb, pan-fried chicken smothered in turmeric, masgoof (grilled fish), and eggplant stews. Women were not allowed in this building.

I was smuggled in once by my male cousins when the men were out. The aroma of coffee grounds and burning wood first met me, then a mix of cigarette smoke and the lingering scents of harvest. The space was unwelcoming for a woman, bare of any feminine touch to soften the scene, and very much a statement of prosperity and heritage. The room was furnished with Arabic-style seating: coarse hand-woven woolen rugs were placed around the room on the floor, with matching cushions here and there for the men to lean on. The walls were hung with the photos of my grandfather and his father and, of course, a diagram of the family tree, which listed only the men. The diagram showed an actual tree, branching out to familiar names and others that were unfamiliar. At the bottom were names going back to the sixth and seventh centuries CE. I followed with my finger a branch that led to my father and then on to the sole leaf that held my brother's name, Haydar.

My Grandmother, Bibi[2]

My grandmother was the backbone of our family. She was married at sixteen to a young man she met only on the day of her wedding, as was the tradition. At that young age, she boldly took on the responsibilities of running a household with her mother-in-law, my paternal great-grandmother.

Amma Amel once told us the story of my grandparents' marriage, which was told to her by her own paternal grandmother. In Iraq, the tradition was (and still is, in some families) that the mother of the groom visits the mother of the bride to decide on the suitability of the match for both families. The union usually depends on the reputations of the families, rather than the choice of the bride and groom, who do not see each other at this stage.

Traditionally, the groom's mother invites other female family

2 The word for grandmother in Iraqi Arabic has many forms: bibi, habooba, and Jedah are some of the most common.

members, including her sisters, close friends and neighbors, to accompany her to visit the bride's mother, propose the idea of a union, and, of course, see the bride. We call this Khitbat al-Niswan—the women's proposal or engagement. This meeting between the mothers decides the next steps for the couple. Sometimes in these meetings a dowry is proposed and future living arrangements are discussed.

My great-grandmother, however, had gone alone to meet my grandmother's family and look at the young woman she would choose for her nineteen-year-old son. She saw a well-mannered young girl, who seemed somewhat shy but capable of taking on the responsibilities of a household. She wore a dark flower-printed dress and had short, very distinct braids coming down to her shoulders, unlike the other women of that time, who wove their hair tightly into one or two thick, dark braids that reached down to their waists and were sometimes adorned at the tips with gold bands.

I recall watching the older women in my family braiding their hair after their baths. Quietly focused, as if meditating, they would smooth out the tangles and meticulously part their hair down the middle to reveal a straight, narrow line of white on the scalp. With each stroke they combed away the anxieties of the day, concentrating only on those dark, wavy strands.

I enjoyed listening to that story about my grandmother. I would imagine her with her short braids, wearing her flowered dress, two small round blue-green tattoos on each of her temples. Women were tattooed for medicinal purposes: to relieve headaches, joint pains, and other maladies. Tattoos, *dagat*, also enhanced a woman's beauty. Some women had dotted tattoo lines trailing the veins on the backs of their hands or from the edge of their bottom lip to the tip of their chin, as my great-grandmother had. When village women came to visit us, I saw some with tattoo lines trailing across their foreheads, outlining their eyebrows and the curves on their faces, others with pyramid-shaped tattoos on their calves. The older women would say that King

Solomon fell in love with the Queen of Sheba when she walked ahead of him with her tattooed calves showing just below the hem of her dress.

Bibi was illiterate; she was never taught to read or write, but she composed folk poetry. Inspired by some feeling or incident, she would call out to one of her children and ask them to write down her lines. The poetry was communal—she would compose a few lines, which then traveled by word of mouth to neighboring homes and villages, until another poet took it upon themselves to answer them. Through puns and witty exchanges, Bibi and her friends composed complete poems starting from a few lines of reflections on love, betrayal, loss, or longing. The poems were read with dramatic intonations and memorized; they were meant to be passed down and remembered through the generations.

Bibi

I see her sitting by the wardrobe, its door ajar.
Her warm and gentle voice
calling out to us.
We would run to her,
our eyes already peeking inside the wardrobe,
looking for that hidden little basket of fruits
and bags of wrapped toffees.
She would fill our palms with sweets,
take in a deep breath, ufaysh[3],
to fill her lungs with the scent of our hair,
as we cuddled against her neck in gratitude.

I see her scrubbing my feet
with a loofah and olive oil soap,
tickling my soles and laughing at my squirms.

I see her in the path of light
floating in from the open oak doors
sitting on the floor, churning butter.

I remember her funeral
and that moment when they brought her coffin home at night,
the women beating their chests in grief,
wailing,
faces red with tears.

Now, to my adult perception
it looks so much like
an angry, passionate dance.
Their long, untamed hair flailing,

---

3   Ufaysh: from Iraqi dialect, a word that reflects happiness and relief, usually said as an endearment.

as they moved slowly,
in a circle
around the coffin,
their arms rising and falling
together, palms
beating their bare chests
with force and purpose

exactly in rhythm
with the mullah's reading,
making music
with their bodies.

The sight is both
chilling and haunting.

I had a cassette tape-
recording of her voice,
the two of us talking
when I was three,
asking questions,
telling me to sing her
nursery rhymes about ducks in a river
ya bat ya bat isbah bilshatt[4].
Her voice soothing, encouraging.

That tape was among the piles
we left behind
when we departed
too quickly to remember
to take everything
we cherish now
                    here in exile.

---

4   little ducks, little ducks, swim in the river.

I was told
that she died because she missed my father,
her chest
was blue and sore
with sorrow that day he left.

Leaving Home

At the beginning of the Iran-Iraq War, my father received a government scholarship to study animal nutrition at the University of
Manitoba. He had wanted to decline the offer, but his father urged
him to accept it. My grandfather already had three sons enlisted in the
Iraqi army. Even though the scholarship would take his fourth son far
away from home and family, at least he would be safe.

My father would have to abandon generations of heritage behind
for an unknown world across the Atlantic. Despite this and the other
journeys he made over the years, he always remained attached to the
home and that tiny village in Iraq where he grew up. His many travels have not changed his Iraqi identity, which lies hidden under his
layers of Western clothes. As soon as he reaches the village outskirts,
he sheds his shirt and pants and puts on his traditional dress; and
he allows that space to welcome and comfort him. He loosens his
Baghdadi dialect and the sounds of his southern Iraqi tongue flow
out. I have often witnessed how his smile broadens as we arrive there;
the dimples in his dark cheerful face deepen the closer we get. He has
a connection to that land and its history; he radiates pride as he gazes
out at its fields.

My father left the comfort of his home and family and traveled to
Canada in 1981; we were to follow him soon after. Before we left to
join him, Bibi passed away.

TWO

———

Winnipeg, Manitoba 1982

The night of our departure for Canada, the family had gathered at the home of my father's older brother, Ammo Mohammad, in Baghdad. My father had left a couple of months before us, in July, to prepare for graduate school and arrange for our arrival, so my mother was traveling alone with three young children, the youngest of whom, my sister Shayma, was eight months old. The street by my uncle's house was jammed with cars of family members who had come to say their farewells. My mother was overwhelmed with repeated goodbyes and all kinds of advice. She was already apprehensive about the separation and isolation, and nervous about what lay ahead for her; it would be her first time on a plane and her first time outside the region. She had had all the help looking after us, now she would be alone.

Her mother, Bibi Masalik, would again and again stuff chicken sandwiches into her handbag. "You and the children will be hungry at the airport," she insisted. My mother politely refused, kissing her mother's hands in gratitude. The scene was emotional and chaotic, with everyone talking and crying all at once. My mother's face was flushed and drawn as she held on to each member of the family. Finally, as our bags were hauled into the trunk of my uncle's car, they embraced each other tightly and I heard my grandmother's whispered prayers for our safe arrival and quick return.

The night we arrived in Winnipeg, after a twenty-four hour journey, my mother's excitement was palpable. She was beginning a new adventure with my father. Yet I sensed also a certain trepidation that restrained her. She had brought with her the news of his mother's death. She had warned us not say anything about it until she had broken the news, and had taken off her black mourning clothes to avoid shocking him at first sight.

My father drove us from the airport to the small, modestly furnished apartment he had rented. There, as my mother unpacked and we rested in the bedroom, he asked her about his family, persisting in his questions about his mother's health. She had been waiting for the right moment, and I could see the tension in her face. I sat watching them as they talked. Somewhere in my head, I knew she was lying to him, and I was eager to tell him about Bibi, but my mother's prior warnings and threats kept me silent.

Suddenly my brother spoke up, "Do you remember how everyone was crying?"

My father turned to my mother and asked, "Is my mother dead?" I heard his voice break as he gazed into her face for an answer.

My mother nodded quietly and bent her head. As he left the room, she glared at me and my brother. "Stay here. Don't leave this room. Didn't I tell you not to say anything?"

She followed him into the living room. After some time, I dared to venture out of the bedroom, and I found my father on the armchair, crying. He wiped the tears from his face when he saw me.

"What's wrong, Baba?" I asked. This was the first time I had seen him cry.

He nodded, drew me toward him, and kissed me on the head. He was staring at the floor, the stream of tears on his face gleaming in the light of the table lamp next to his chair. I think he sobbed a couple of times, but then stopped when he remembered my presence. His grief was greater because in this foreign city, far from family, he could not properly express it; he did not take part in the funeral or witness her burial.

My mother pushed me back into the bedroom and closed the door.

Shortly after, while he was studying, my father wrote a poem for his mother and stuffed it into the pocket of his robe. He found it still there a few years later. Every time my mother washed the robe, she had made sure to remove the paper first and then carefully return it into the pocket later.

———

In Manitoba, my brother and I were placed in kindergarten and the first grade, respectively; we were young and easily picked up the language and made friends at school. My parents, on the other hand, had to adjust to a new life with many challenges, such as language, lack of a community, and of course the bitter winters. While my father worked through his courses, my mother learned to adapt. She would say that God had sent down a piece of heaven and placed it in Canada. When we traveled out west to Banff and Vancouver in the summer, she was amazed at the green fields, the mountains, and the clear lakes that came into view.

Through his courses at the university, my father befriended a group of young Iraqi students, who became like family to us. My mother would invite them over for dolma and biryani, and after our meal they would stay on for the rest of the evening, singing Iraqi songs throughout the night with turned-over pots as tablas. They were our young uncles who would babysit me and my siblings, take us on outings, and build with us red and yellow Lego houses that we never wanted to disassemble. Our photographs from those days in Winnipeg remind us of the joyful times we spent with these students on trips, in parks, and sitting together around meals. Nevertheless, my mother's longing for home was overwhelming. She lost her father six months after our arrival in Canada, and the Iran-Iraq war kept her anxious about her family and friends. I can only imagine the sense of *ghurba* she felt. The winter days were the worst, when she felt like she was suffocating in that apartment and it had become a prison. She would desperately try to crack open a window to breathe in fresh outdoor air, pulling hard at the frozen pane, to no avail.

———

My mother was the youngest of seven siblings in a loving, close-knit family. Originally from the holy city of Najaf, her family moved to Karadat Mariam in Baghdad a year before she was born. She grew up in the fifties and sixties, at a time when revolutions sprang up like weeds. Iraq was in constant turmoil as different political forces—pro-British politicians, Nationalists, the Iraqi Communist Party, and the Arab Ba'ath Socialist Party—fought to gain control of the country. Her family were socialists, believing in a society with equal opportunities for all. They read Arabic and Western authors, wrote poetry, and were knowledgeable in history, literature, and politics; shelves of books filled their homes. But their socialist views made them targets for the Iraqi government. She would speak about family members being imprisoned and tortured. Due to growing violence, her older brothers were discouraged from leaving the house; instead, she would be sent out to the baker's to buy bread, since as a girl she would be the least likely to be detained or attacked if riots or street fights broke out. She would push the money under the door and wait for the baker to quickly open it to pass her the stack of khubuz.

Due to the constant threats, her father, a goldsmith, decided to leave the country with a couple of his cousins. For five years, her older brothers took care of the family and found ways to support their mother and their four sisters. Her father's departure did not change the fact that they were still targeted by police. Officers would come looking for my uncles and they had to be smuggled from one house to another. Their father's sister, Um Saad, lived next door and sometimes she would hide them in her home. She was a courageous woman and once, when they were taken by the police she went to the station to argue for their release. She succeeded.

Another Move and Another Adjustment

My father completed his master's degree after two years and was accepted in a doctoral program at Washington State University. In February 1985, we drove across the Rocky Mountains in our light-green Chevrolet Impala towing a small U-Haul trailer to Pullman, Washington.

Here my mother felt more comfortable and independent; her English was better and she obtained her driving licence. She also found new ways to keep herself busy while we were at school: she took up sewing and attended craft classes and women's gatherings at an international women's association. My parents even rented a garden plot near our house where they grew vegetables. She would spend hours planting and weeding, and our fridge began to overflow with oversized beefsteak tomatoes and zucchini. She also made friends outside of the very limited circle of Iraqis that we knew. She seemed settled and happy.

My father took some of the summers off from courses and research and we traveled by car sometimes down to California and sometimes as far west as Washington DC and New York. He would plan our routes on AAA maps, with surprise stops for us on the way. Equipped with our rust-colored five-people tent and a cooler, we camped under the Redwoods in California, or woke up licking the salt from our lips off the shores of the Atlantic, or slept in the backyard camping grounds of cheap motels. My parents loved traveling and they made sure we saw as much of the United States as possible.

Sometimes we stayed with Iraqi families on the way. Once, on our way to Disneyland, we stayed with an Iraqi family in Oregon, and they made *batcha* and *bumbarat*—sheep's head and lamb intestines stuffed with rice and spices—both Iraqi delicacies. I watched with disgust as my mother and our hostess prepared the meal, cleaning the head and intestines, the sheep's eyes looking back at them and the tongue hanging out to the side between stained teeth. Through these visits, my parents had the opportunity to socialize with other Iraqis and exchange news about home, while Haydar, Shayma, and I learned a little more about our culture and practiced our Arabic.

During our seven years abroad, none of us except my father visited Iraq. He went to see his father, who had had a massive stroke. When he returned to Pullman, he said that the country had changed and he was hesitant to take us back. People were tired from the long war with Iran and the political scene was disturbing. Portraits and statues of Saddam Hussein were on display everywhere, in the streets, shops, and offices. My parents briefly contemplated staying on in the United States.

THREE

My parents claim that the leading reason for their return to Iraq was me. I was turning thirteen and they dreaded the thought of raising a teenage girl in a Western society, away from our culture and traditions. I was growing up North American, but with traditional parents, and I saw their anxieties over things that I felt were trivial. My father found my shorts too short and my skirts too tight. My mother began to talk about Iraqi society and what was required of "young ladies" my age. Our talks usually began with inquiries about my friends and their boyfriends and ended up with warnings about how girls in our culture never had boyfriends. It was shameful and dishonorable for a family to have "loose" girls who were in relationships, so I was not allowed to go to slumber parties, school dances, or the mall. I was constrained to our neighborhood and to the families we knew. All this meant that I felt left out and different.

In her exhortations, my mother conveniently left out the fact that she and my father had fallen in love at university and been in a very public relationship. When I was older I was able to sift through their black-and-white university photographs of picnics, trips, and parties, my mother's beautiful face framed by her long, dark hair and my handsome father in his 1970s bell-bottoms. Once, she showed us the journal they had kept together. They would take it with them during holidays and breaks and fill it with their thoughts, their experiences, and their dreams for the future. Although Iraqi society at the time was more liberated, people were still somewhat conservative; the notebook allowed them some freedom to share their feelings for each other. They kept this habit of writing in the journal even after their marriage, recording what they felt to be some of the most important moments in their lives.

On my most recent birthday, my dad sent me an entry from that journal that documented my birth. The first few sentences, loosely translated, say: "On this bright day of winter, the first fruit of our love was born. She has a bright face and lovely features. She was born in Al-Furat al-Awsat hospital in Al-Kufa. I named her Lamees because the name is rare and close to my heart. Both her mother and I feel she is a good omen."

Baghdad 1988

My mother, my two siblings, and I returned to Baghdad on December 9 1988, four months after the end of the Iran-Iraq War. My father stayed behind in Washington for a few months to complete his graduation requirements.

Our entire extended family was at the airport, waiting for us when we landed: aunts, uncles, cousins, my mother's cousins, and their spouses. My mother left our baggage and paperwork in the hands of my father's brothers and floated toward her family, who were on the other side of the arrivals gate. It had been seven years since she last saw them, she had missed births, deaths, and weddings. Through the thick glass doors, she made signs to inquire about the children's names, and my aunts mouthed out the names through their tears. Haydar, Shayma, and I looked on in amazement at the number of people who had come out to welcome us and their displays of emotion.

After the paperwork was complete, the glass doors slid open and we were drowned in embraces and greetings. Ammo Shakir took me aside and asked me to guess the names of all my cousins, calling out to them one by one to come greet me. I felt lost in this tumultuous crowd of relatives, young and old, but I was also thrilled. I felt that I was finally home, in the home my parents had been talking about and missing all the years we had been away. That night everyone gathered at Amma Amel's house. She had prepared dinner for the whole family.

Afterward, my mother and I went to my mother's oldest brother Khalo[5] Abass's house. I did not sleep that night, staying up with my mom as she talked about the changes she noticed, how much older everyone looked, and how happy she felt that she was finally back home. We counted the chimes on the grandfather clock in the

5   Khalo means maternal uncle.

hallway and listened to the roosters in the backyard waking up the neighborhood.

———

Even with all the happiness that we felt upon our return, our relatives soon began to relate their struggles over the past years. Due to conscription, all my uncles had served in the military; their hearts were heavy with the losses of friends and family members. We had returned to a country reeling from a destructive war and trying, with difficulty, to regain the stability and prosperity of the 1970s. My memories of the Iran-Iraq War were very limited. When the war began, we were living in the city of Basra. I remember my mother moving around the house, closing drapes and turning off lights when the sirens announced an airstrike.

While we were in Canada and the US, my father would be glued to the television to see the news. He would shout at us to quiet down as he heard the latest developments taking place back home. We would watch the grave look on his face as the news anchor listed areas that were attacked and the most recent numbers of casualties.

There had been conflicts between Iraq and Iran long before the war, over land and Shatt al-Arab, the river in which the Tigris and Euphrates meet in the south of Iraq and the only Iraqi waterway with access to the Arab Gulf. The clashing political agendas of Saddam Hussein in Iraq and Ayatollah Khomeini in Iran, who both rose to power in 1979, in addition to foreign interference and interests in the region, all had a role to play in the conflagration that became the eight-year war that led to the loss of hundreds of thousands of lives and put the country billions of dollars in debt.

In the news we saw prisoners of war disembark from airplanes, their bodies like shadows in ragged clothes, their heads shaven. So lifeless, they looked like they had left their souls behind. They would reach the tarmac and kneel to kiss the ground and cry. For some families the men who returned had changed beyond recognition, physically and mentally. The years in Iranian prisons had left them traumatized and anxious; some were disconnected from the communities they returned to and others were angry and discontent. They had lost their jobs, their families, and years from their lives. There were soldiers who had been missing in action or declared dead, who returned back to find that their wives had remarried or left the country.

Unknown Soldiers

The first image of an Iraqi soldier that I clearly recall was in a picture I saw when I was ten. As a student on a government scholarship, my father had to remain connected to developments back home. He had received a pamphlet from the Iraqi government showing Iraqi prisoners of war in Iran. The front of the folded pamphlet showed a man's face twisted into an agonizing scream, his eyes shut tight. When I unfolded the glossy paper, I saw that the man's arm had been torn off. I could see the tear in his sleeve, but the arm was not there. I was so horrified, I could not swallow.

I had found something I was not supposed to see. When I showed the pamphlet to my mother, she asked me nervously, "Where did you find it?"

"It was on the record player. What is happening to that man in the picture, Mama? Where is his arm? Have they cut it with a sword?"

She tried to deflect me, but I would not give up. Finally she relented.

"They tie the arms of the captured soldiers to trucks that move in opposite directions," she finally said. She looked away.

I struggled for years to push back that image. I would wake up from nightmares in which my father's face had replaced that of the soldier in the photograph. He was being tortured by faceless men in trucks. As I write this now, that same feeling crawls up my throat, the man's face still clear in my mind.

Even after the war, television channels continued to show images from the battlefront and singers praising Saddam Hussein's leadership and the bravery of our fallen heroes. We would see Saddam at the front shooting rifles or handling heavy artillery, surrounded by soldiers chanting his name. In the early evening, before the children's hour, a show titled *Suar Min al-Maarakah*—Images from the Battle— would come on. For half an hour we were exposed to images of dead and mutilated Iranian soldiers on the front, while some classical tune played in the background.

My parents found life extremely complicated as they tried to re-adapt to a life they no longer understood or belonged to. During their time in Canada and the States, they had established a life independent of their relatives. In those seven years abroad, my parents had made sure that we followed schedules for meals, homework, and bed times. But back in Iraq our cousins ate whenever they liked and slept at late hours, after watching movies my parents had prohibited us from seeing.

Moreover, our little family had to split. My father was obligated to teach at the University of Basra in southern Iraq, from which he had graduated. My parents had in fact met there, and Basra was an important part of their youthful romantic years. But nothing was left of their beloved city, it had been destroyed beyond recognition, having been one of the main battlegrounds during the eight years of war with Iran. At the beginning of each week, my father would drive down six hours to Basra, and then return to spend one weekend night with us, tired and disillusioned. The image of the future that he had built for his family over the years had disintegrated into this unwelcoming reality that his homeland had become.

I saw my parents struggling with the burdens of a life they had for-gotten, dealing with a society that had grown coarse in their absence. The energetic, high-spirited life that I had known with my parents abroad was gone. My mother looked constantly depleted, being busy with furnishing and establishing our new home in Baghdad, where everything seemed strange now.

Baghdad 1989

At first my siblings and I had felt like we were on vacation. Family members came to visit us or take us out to see the city. One day Ammo Mohammad took us out for lunch.

"What would you like to eat?" he called out to us from the front seat.

We negotiated options amongst ourselves and concluded that we missed McDonald's the most. So we agreed on hamburgers. Ammo Mohammad said he knew just the place. We parked in front of the restaurant called Al-Sayyar. The entrance was of white marble and glass; inside, everything was also marble: the columns, the tables, and the order counter. We had been Americanized, or as Iraqis say "Mitamrikeen," and we felt completely out of place. Our expectations of restaurants were limited to the fast-food places our parents had allowed us to eat at every once in a while.

We stepped up to the counter and ordered burgers.

The man who took our order was Egyptian. He peered down at us, smiled with a full toothy grin, and asked, "Batatis?"

We stared at him in confusion. He asked us again, "Batatis?"

Finally, both my uncle and the man laughed out loud. "He is asking you if you want potatoes," my uncle clarified. "They don't speak Arabic," he explained to the employee.

The man's Egyptian dialect sounded like a completely different language to me. In time, with the overflow of Egyptian television programs and movies we would pick it up. The burgers came carefully wrapped in white paper, along with hot and greasy "batatis" that smelled divine. But the burgers were far from the McDonald's burgers we had anticipated. The buns were plate-sized, more like brioches, and the patties inside were small. They were covered with something like steak sauce and gave off a distinct smell of garlic; they were nothing like the burgers we were used to. We ate as much as we could to please our uncle, who laughed and teased us.

Ketchup, mustard, peanut butter, and other food staples that we were used to in the States were rare and expensive. My mother tried her best to find alternatives, but even with her creative culinary abilities, she was very limited. Other issues that seemed too trivial for our cousins began to break us down. We were constantly teased for being too soft and spoilt, too Americanized. For us, these issues were cataclysmic. Our schools lacked air-conditioning in the early summer and heating in the winter. We would either freeze in the classrooms or faint from the heat. Dust was everywhere and we would return home covered in it. On windy days, it got into our hair and our mouths.

Then there were the political parades and rallies. They were never announced beforehand, perhaps because the authorities feared that we would not show up if we knew about them. Soon after I began to attend school, all the kids were taken on buses to a rally supporting Saddam Hussein and his visitor, King Fahd of Saudi Arabia. We were dumped on the side of the airport highway and stood about aimlessly, waiting for the president's drive-by. After several hours of extreme heat, thirst, and hunger, some kids began to faint. Ambulances arrived to care for them, and trucks came with armed soldiers to pass (or throw) oranges to us. I remember going with one of my classmates to beg for water from one of the bus drivers. He was out of clean water, but he managed to give us some from the bottle he used to service the bus; it tasted foul, but we were grateful.

In the States, I had close friends and my grades were above average; I played the violin, took interest in art, and felt confident. In Baghdad, I struggled with all my schoolwork and the cultural restrictions that dictated what I could wear and how I should act. I felt that I had to become someone else to be accepted by my schoolmates. Teenage boys catcalled or whistled at me, as they did at other girls, as I walked to school and back. I felt vulnerable every time I left the house. And so I looked for excuses to stay home. I stopped wearing knee-length shorts and skirts, and I learned to walk with my head down to avoid eye contact whenever possible. I still tend to do that sometimes, and I have to remind myself that I have long outgrown that thirteen-year-old Iraqi girl and her fears.

Students in Iraqi schools were extremely competitive. I faced a lot of difficulty because my Arabic was weak. I understood everything that was taught, but I could not put together comprehensible sentences. Some of my teachers, like my geography teacher, Miss Sahar, understood my predicament. She would sit next to me and ask me to answer the questions orally, then she would write down the answers so that I would receive a mark for my knowledge of the material. But not all of them understood or cared about my situation. One day, while writing a science exam at school, a substitute teacher peered over my shoulder and found that I had not been correcting the false statements in the True or False portion, as was required.

"What do you think you're doing?" she yelled and struck me across the face. I started sobbing into my hands. My whole world seemed to have ended right there in that humiliating moment. I could not stop crying. Another teacher came up to the doorway to see what had happened. The substitute replied sarcastically that all she had done was slap me; the second teacher replied that I was a newcomer from abroad and did not know the system.

"That's enough," she said to me with a laugh. "It was only a slap!"

On the long walk home, I kept telling myself that my mother would take care of everything, maybe even get the teacher fired. But she would not even talk to the teacher or the principal. Ammo Mohammad was visiting and, tearfully, I told him about the incident. He was so upset that immediately he began to head out to the school to speak with the principal.

"I will get that teacher fired!" he shouted. I felt a rush of relief that justice would be done. But my mother restrained him.

"We don't want trouble with the school," she said. "Why should Lamees be treated differently from other students in her classroom? It's normal practice here."

I stared at my mother and said quietly, "Mama, let him go please." But I knew I would lose this argument.

She and my uncle looked at me with concern, then my uncle sat back down on the couch. I went to my room.

Gradually, I lost the motivation to study. My mother tried her best to help me, but I simply shut down. I lost confidence in myself and stopped communicating with my parents.

That year I failed in Arabic, Islamic Studies, civics, and math. I was at my Aunt Hanna's house when my parents came, wearing somber looks. They sat me down in the kitchen and told me that I had been held back in the seventh grade. Something broke inside me and, unconsciously, I released a high-pitched scream. I ran upstairs and hid under the bathroom sink. I could not bear anyone to see me. I was embarrassed and felt that I had let myself and my parents down.

Samarra 1990

A few months later, my father found a position at a branch of the Ministry of Agriculture that did research in his field of expertise. He moved us once again, this time to the ancient city of Samarra, which was the capital of the Abbasid Caliphate around the ninth century. A new city had grown around the remains of the ancient capital, and two holy shrines, of Ali al-Hadi and Hassan al-Askari, were embedded right in its heart. According to some Shia beliefs, the shrine is also where Mohammed al-Mahdi or Sahib al-Zaman disappeared; it is believed that his reemergence will signal the coming of the Apocalypse.

In Samarra, I found myself again. The people of Samarra were kind and down-to-earth; I easily made friends and began to enjoy going to school. We went on picnics on the banks of the Dijla[6] and visited the numerous archeological sites—I remember in particular Dar al-Khilafa, the Caliphal Palace, which had dimly-lit hallways and a massive pool in the center. We would go on school trips to the Al-Ashique (the Lover) and Al-Ma'shooque (the Beloved) Palaces, where we would try to imagine the Caliph's journey through the long underground tunnel between the two palaces, leading him to his beloved. From our driveway we could see the ancient Great Mosque, one of the largest in the world, and the famous Malwiya Minaret—the spiraling minaret, fifty-two meters high.

Malwiya Minaret in Samarra

With my father's new job and the comfort of having the whole family under one roof, we finally found a sense of settlement. We regained some closeness, and our lives became organized once again around set schedules.

Unfortunately, we were soon thrust into the trauma of the first Gulf War.

6   The Tigris River.

The Gulf War, Baghdad 1990

I was woken by the radio playing patriotic war songs against the distinct voice of the lead Iraqi news anchor in the background. We were on our summer vacation and I was staying at my Amma Amel's house in Baghdad. I found her in the kitchen ironing an army tunic. She let out a forceful sigh and mumbled something under her breath, as a dark brown burn mark appeared on the collar.

"Good morning, Amma. What's wrong?" I asked quietly.

"He attacked Kuwait," she replied, not looking up. "Your uncle Abd has been called for duty."

Beads of sweat had gathered on her forehead. My father's oldest sibling was a very strong woman. She had helped raise her brothers and sisters, taught herself to read because she was not able to attend school; she had survived six miscarriages, the turmoil of several Iraqi revolutions and political upheavals, and the eight-year war against Iran. But at that moment, she looked shattered. Carefully gliding the iron up and down that shirt was probably the only thing keeping her from breaking down.

God was merciful, but the times were beyond comprehension once again.

As the day wore on, a quiet commotion spread across the city. The two television channels continuously played patriotic songs of support and love for the Leader. People everywhere spoke in whispers to each other, exchanging news and speculations. The hot, dusty air felt like a physical presence that sat perversely on our chests.

When I returned to school in Samarra, we were taught safety training for possible air raids, which included lessons in making gas masks from flannel and coal. All the windows of our house were crossed with box tape and covered with plastic sheets for protection against shrapnel and poison gas. All our assemblies began with speeches condemning the American government and vows of fighting the coalition attacks.

Samarra, January 17 1991

When the Coalition air raids began on Samarra, we were all gathered in my bedroom. My mother's older sister, Khala[7] Hanna, had come down with her family from Baghdad, expecting Samarra to be safer. The sirens had sounded only moments before. The house was dark, and headlights from the cars on the road outside formed flitting shadows on the curtains. I imagined soldiers crouching outside our windows. I had not been aware that the invasion would come mostly by air and sea.

I, my two siblings, and my cousins, Rafif and Raneen, huddled together chatting softly as the bombers roared and shrieked overhead. We felt calm and were somewhat enjoying the sense of danger, as if we were in the midst of an adventure. What I remember most were the queues we had to join to use our only bathroom; we all seemed to have urges to go at the same time. As soon as everyone had had their turn, the line would form again. It seemed hilarious, but obviously we were much more afraid than we believed.

Our house was located close to the Samarra Drugs Factory, the state pharmaceutical manufacturer. Suspected of making chemical weapons, it was one of the main targets of the missiles. As the night wore on, our excitement turned to terror. Our mothers prayed constantly, reading verses from the Quran and invoking God's name repeatedly, "Ya Allah, Ya Allah, Ya Allah." After a sleepless night, my father packed us and Khala Hanna's family in the car and drove us to my grandfather's house in Al-Harmia, hoping it would prove safer.

Al-Harmia 1991

At my grandfather's home, we were without electricity or running water. My aunts and my mother kept everything moving in a timely fashion and found creative ways to cook meals to save on gas and

---

7   Khala means maternal aunt; it is also used when addressing older women.

kerosene. They made sure the food was rationed to last as long as possible and tried different recipes with whatever ingredients the men brought from neighboring stores and towns. We were all assigned chores to keep us busy and help with keeping the house in order. A routine began to form:

Wake up.

Cook breakfast.

Eat.

Wait for the men to bring in water from the river.

Fill the barrels in the house with the water.

Boil the water.

Sweep.

Mop.

Clean the kerosene lamps and heaters.

Fill the lamps with kerosene.

Fill the heaters with kerosene.

Cook.

Eat.

Clean.

Sleep.

The house was crowded with twenty-eight people living in it; in addition, neighbors and relatives dropped in daily to visit and share meals. So many of us were teenagers: I had cousins from both sides of the family, and Amma Amel's neighbors, who had come with her from Baghdad, had also brought along their teenage children. We divided ourselves according to age groups and spent most of the day finishing up chores and helping with meals. We broke the routine by visiting neighbors or taking slow car rides at night to Alibadi, the only shop around, about five minutes away.

The short trips to the tiny, boxlike shop were our escape from the hectic and stifling atmosphere of the house. We stayed out as long as we could, that is, until the air raids began again. Our music turned high and the windows rolled up, we would see the sky light up first, followed by the sound of explosions.

Back in the house, we would gather around the kerosene heaters and tell jokes and stories, trying our best to get through the long winter nights. Winters in Iraq reach zero Celsius and sometimes a few degrees below. On colder nights we would wake up to see a dusting of frost on the grass, but it quickly disappeared with the morning sun. The cold air was dry and reached into the marrow of our bones. Our brick-and-concrete houses were colder inside, even though the rooms and hallways were equipped with heaters. In flannel pajamas or nightgowns, wearing socks and wrapped in robes and shawls, we would still be shivering as we hurried through the hallways to the bathroom. Sometimes the bathroom would have a small Ala al-Deen heater with a pot of simmering water on top to mix with the cold water for washing hands. If not, we would wash with cold water from the buckets and endure the stings from the cuts on our dry, chapped hands.

My grandmother's old room, small and cozy, was always the best place to gather. The girls would sit on the floor gossiping while the boys made shadow figures by the light of the kerosene lamp in the room. We only stopped for the sounds of approaching jets, holding our breaths. If the planes passed, we went back to our conversations, but if an attack began we scattered toward our parents. Each of us dealt with the sounds of missiles differently: some of us were silent, trying desperately to hold it together, others quietly cried and recited verses from the Quran.

Because of the distance to neighboring towns, it was difficult to get proper medical care. One day my cousin Lubna and I were helping in the kitchen grinding beef cubes and potatoes in the manual meat grinder, when my father passed by and made a joke. We began laughing with him. I looked down to push a cube of potato into the grinder, when my cousin inadvertently turned the handle. I screamed with pain, as my index and middle fingers got gripped in the auger. My father rushed to me and gently pulled out my hand. My two fingers were intact, but their tips looked badly mauled, both the fingernails crushed. All the adults gathered around sympathetically to inspect my fingers and blew on them and wrapped them to stop the bleeding. I was given something to calm my nerves and take away the pain and spent the rest of the day tucked into a bed in Bibi's room. There was nothing else anyone could do.

But my ordeal was little compared to what my aunt Mariam suffered. In a hospital in Al-Mishkhab, a nearby town, she gave birth under a heavy air raid and a power outage. She had a Caesarean section, like all her previous births, but without effective anesthetic she remained awake throughout the procedure. In the midst of it, the attending doctor, a woman, was informed that her family home had been bombed, so she left Amma Mariam in the middle of the operation and ran out. The nurses had to take over the delivery. She and the baby survived, but it took them a long time to regain their strength.

Al-Harmia, February 27-28 1991

The atmosphere in the country grew more and more tense. My father and uncles would sit huddled together on floor mats, listening to Radio Monte Carlo blaring out news broadcasts; they seemed to have lost their minds, shouting at the each other, at the radio, at us. They had survived and adapted to numerous changes in their lives, they had protected their lands and their families from multiple changes of regimes. Now they argued if Saddam's government would fall, and what to do to protect the family if American and Coalition forces invaded our homes. I remember one night in particular. The men were exhausted by their own arguments, their faces were grim and looked distorted from the dancing flames of the kerosene lamps.

Bush Senior's voice came on, announcing the ceasefire. It was February 28.

The first Gulf War ended on a dark and damp night.
Bush Sr spoke "ceasefire"
on the radio
while the jets roared and screamed overhead.
The airstrikes shook the dust
between the cracks in the brick walls.
It was raining, or it had been raining
the porch was covered with puddles,
which we sidestepped as we ran out of the house.
They moved my grandfather out into the cold.
He had survived a stroke,
but was struggling with hemiparesis.
He couldn't object, but his eyes kept straying
back toward the warmth of the house.
Then, the sky lit up
with two massive globes
suspended in the air.
We watched
the fighter jets dive,
strike down line
after line
of retreating Iraqi soldiers
at the borders of our land.
None of us said a word,
only stared up at the exploding sky.
I am not sure what we were waiting for.

We later learned that the American army had been using for the first time ammunition containing depleted uranium. An estimated 300 tons of it was used in that war, an opportunity apparently for the Americans to test their weapons in their exercise of military power [8].

8   "The Use of Radioactive Weapons Against the 'Iraqi Enemy'," Naïma Lefkir-Laffitte & Roland Laffite, Trans. W.E. Griffin, 1995.

The Uprising

A few days before the ceasefire, we began hearing disturbing news from the holy city of Najaf, home of Imam Ali's shrine. People there had begun to speak out openly against Saddam's government. In my young mind, speaking against Saddam Hussein was blasphemous. We had been taught never to criticize him in any manner. Like many Iraqis, I feared him more than God. We had heard stories about entire families being imprisoned, tortured, or executed for trivial reasons like telling a joke about Saddam or commenting about one of his speeches.

When news began to reach us about problems in cities nearby, our family became cautious. One day, while we were driving back along the riverside from a relative's house, a man came running out of the reeds; his lightly colored dishdasha was covered in blood and he begged my father for a ride. "A grenade went off and my friend is injured. Please help us!" he stuttered. The hem of his dishdasha was wrapped around his waist, and his entire body was shivering. Sweat dripped down from his face. I looked from my father's concerned face to the bloodstains on the man's clothes. My father calmly told him that he would send help as soon as possible and drove away. This was no time to trust anybody or to be seen to take sides.

A few days later Bibi Masalik, my maternal grandmother, was pushed down by men carrying rifles inside the Imam Ali shrine in Najaf. For Shias, it is forbidden even to carry weapons in that sacred space. The men were shouting slogans against the government and praise for the Shia Imams—words that had led to executions and exiles of so many people over the years.

The shrine became the headquarters of the uprising. On the microphones, usually used to call for prayer (the adhan), names were announced of men who were loyal to Saddam Hussein's government; then they were hunted down and butchered in the shrine. The stories that began to circulate about the uprising were horrific. One man reported that the blood of the tortured and murdered men flowed on the marble floors of the shrine, and he had to lift his abaya to avoid it getting soiled.

The uprising might have begun with a revolt against a tyrant, but soon it turned into a form of vengeance against those who had worked for the government or were members of the Ba'ath party. Much worse was the Iraqi government's retaliation against the "rebellious mobs," as they were labeled. Years later, we would learn the fates of the many who were caught in the confrontations between the rebels and the government.

Many families migrated from the larger cities to rural areas and villages in order to escape the violence. My grandfather and my uncles took in over one hundred and fifty people. They built tents around their houses and set up outdoor kitchens; they fed and cared for the refugee families for about a month, using all their resources to keep them safe.

———

The day after the ceasefire, my father decided that we should return to Baghdad. As a government employee, he could easily be considered a traitor by his superiors and his colleagues if he stayed away any longer. Once again, he crammed us and Khala Hanna and her family into the car and we headed toward Baghdad. We avoided Najaf and decided to go through Karbala instead, hoping to stay clear of whatever was taking place there. But Karbala, another holy city, with the shrines of the martyred Imam al-Hussein and Imam al-Abbas, was no better. People there looked agitated. A man on the street shouted a string of curses at Saddam Hussein. We were stunned at this and other very public displays of disgust and anger. I asked my father about what we had just heard and he told me to keep quiet.

We left the city limits in silence.

On the way, we watched the retreating remnants of the Iraqi army, tanks and trucks lining the road as far as the eye could see. Previously a symbol of courage and pride, now they reflected defeat and anguish. We rolled down the windows and cheered the soldiers manning them; we made symbols of victory with our hands. Their weary faces were covered with dust; they shook their heads at us in reply.

One of them, however, smiled, perhaps at our naiveté. That image of the Iraqi soldier is imprinted in my mind: his thick black mustache, the slight lift at the corners of his lips, the black eyes that hid so much pain.

We Move Again

For the next few months, we lived with Khala Hanna—my mother's sister—and her husband Ammo Sami at their house in Baghdad. My aunt was a renowned artist; her pottery attracted buyers even from outside the country and she had designed and built a mural for Basra International Airport, which is still there today. Her home was like a museum, with pieces of art on the walls and shelves. She would change the color scheme and furniture in her house every two years. I loved her house. We always had freedom there to do whatever we liked. She would wake up dancing and singing, make us breakfast, then gather us in her old, battered silver Datsun to go shopping or visit relatives across the city. We would spend hours working in her pottery studio, learning how to make our own unique creations.

During the air raids, her face would turn pale, and the wrinkles around her mouth and eyes would deepen. She would sway like a palm leaf in a storm as she sobbed and wailed in terror. We feared she would lose her mind or have a heart attack. When we returned to Baghdad she seemed to have settled back into her fun-loving, carefree self.

We still had about three months of school left, so my parents enrolled Haydar and Shayma in my cousin Raneen's primary school across the street, while my cousin Rafif and I attended her all-girls middle school. Although we were all packed inside the two-bedroom home, we welcomed the change and the return to Baghdad. The local community was friendly and supportive; neighbors would drop by for coffee or share a plate of whatever they had cooked that day. My mother was about a year and a half younger than my aunt and they had grown up like friends. The atmosphere was calmer and quieter than what we had recently experienced at the height of the war.

My mother and Khala Hanna learned to bake bread on Ala al-Deen kerosene heaters; the round narrow heaters were perfect for baking pita bread. Ammo Sami would use the car battery to generate power for the light bulbs, when we needed to complete our homework, or the television.

After a few months my father was finally given accommodation in Baghdad and we moved into a house on the banks of the Dijla.

Living Through the Sanctions

The UN-imposed sanctions on Iraq began before the Gulf War, on August 6 1990. Intended to pressure the Iraqi government, the embargo only impacted the well-being of Iraqi people, who suffered tremendously due to the shortages of food and medical supplies. With continuing inflation and reduced employment, the country was heading toward catastrophe.

The report "Health and Welfare in Iraq After the Gulf Crisis: An In-depth Assessment" (1991) states,

> Unless Iraq quickly obtains food, medicine, and spare parts, millions of Iraqis will continue to experience malnutrition and disease. Children by the tens of thousands will remain in jeopardy. Thousands will die.

> [I]t is estimated that the mortality rate of children under five years of age is 380 percent greater today than before the onset of the Gulf Crisis.

The Gulf Peace Team report "Generator Assessment and Installation Project" (1991) on the Saddam Hussein Central Children's Hospital relates,

> This hospital was a [sic] full capacity before the war began in January 1991. On or around the first day of the war, 90% of the patients left.

> 40-50 children died in the hospital in the first few hours of bombing. The weather was cold and mothers took their children into the basement, where there was no heat.

Another report by the Gulf Peace Team adds,

> The country has been paralyzed due to near-complete loss in its electricity generating capacity. Without electricity, water pumping stations are dormant. Sewage is left untreated. Industries are closed down (levels of unemployment have reached 70-90 percent). Fuel for cooking and transportation is unavailable. Hospitals are merely reservoirs of infection since most medicines are in short supply, laboratories cannot function, operating theatres have no supplies, and basic services are unavailable.

> Food is prohibitively expensive and generally in scarce supply.

> Displacement of the civilian population, in both the south and the north, has greatly aggravated post-war conditions. Refugees and other internally-displaced civilians are at greatest risk of ill-health and mortality.

> Since August 1990, the Iraqi government has been prohibited from purchasing or importing any quantity of foodstuffs for civilian consumption. This represents the first time that a sovereign state has been prohibited from importing food for its own people.

Simple items like white flour and sugar became scarce. People were given monthly rations and we witnessed the divide between social classes become deeper as families began to live on the bare minimum.

The government Food Ration Card[9] contained a message for Iraqi women from Saddam Hussein:

To the Majidat[10]

- When the economic lifestyle is organized according to the program we have devised, the battle will be won for Iraq and the Arab Nation.
- What I ask of you today is to organize your family's economic lifestyle.
- In your cooking pots and on your dinning tables, the food you cook should only be what is actually needed to sustain your family.

President Saddam Hussein

جمهورية العراق
وزارة التجارة
بطاقة تموين
١٩٩٩
بغداد
الرقم

الى الماجدات

● عندما تنتظم الحياة الاقتصادية وفق البرنامج الذي ننشده تكون المعركة قد انحسمت لصالح العراق والامة

● ان الدور الذي اناشدك ايتها الماجدة القيام به اليوم هو تنظيم الحياة الاقتصادية للاسرة .

● المطلوب ان تكون كميات الغذاء الموضوعة في القدور وعلى المائدة بقدر ما نحتاج فعلاً للحياة الجديدة .

الرئيس القائد صدام حسين

---

9   Barbara Nimri Aziz kindly provided me with these sources regarding the embargo and sanctions.
10   Majidat was used by Hussein and the Iraqi government to refer to Iraqi women, describing them as diligent.

The rations covered the following items: flour, rice, vegetable oil, sugar, tea, legumes, salt, soap, detergent, and baby formula. The rice was usually old, with a stale moldy smell, and flour was dark and grainy and contained wheat hulls, stones, and sticks, which made the bread tough, dark, and too hard to bite into. The cheaper flour, which was imported from different sources, sometimes seemed to be mixed with sawdust.

Some families lived on as little as three dollars a month, selling family heirlooms and antiques to survive. A family friend began to secretly sell furniture, art, and household items he had collected during his years of travels abroad. Another family was robbed while they were out of the house. The intruders took only the bags of rice and flour that were in the pantry; unfortunately, the family's jewelry was hidden in those bags. But the next day a tearful man came to return the jewelry, saying that he only intended to take the food for his children.

While the middle class began selling their assets, the less fortunate ones sent out their children into the streets to do labor and to sell whatever they could to passersby and cars that stopped at the traffic lights.

Stories of hardship and suffering proliferated. We whispered them to each other in the school hallways; if we were overheard, we would be punished. To portray images of privation was considered a declaration of defeat. As teenagers, we missed our junk food; it was nearly impossible to find it, local or imported. The few candy and cola factories that remained open used dates to sweeten their products, and the taste was sometimes unbearable. Later some small shops began to import things like candy bars, soda, and chips, but the prices were ridiculously high and unattainable for most people.

The dynamics of the Iraqi home altered as more women began to work and men began to leave the country in search of jobs and better living conditions for their families. While traditional values adjusted to give women more freedom, at the same time people began to observe stricter religious practices. Women who had been *saferat* (without hijab) began to wear headscarves and gave up makeup. Many people turned reclusive.

FOUR

———

Dijla

I would sit on the rooftop of my parents' house on Abu Nuwas Street at night watching the bright silvery moon courting Dijla. During Ramadan, just before Adhan al-Maghrib—the call for the sunset prayer—I would see the gently flowing water soaking up the last rays of sunlight in hues of violet and orange.

Dijla—the Tigris—runs through the most crowded parts of Baghdad, splitting the ancient city into two main districts, Al-Karkh and Al-Rasafa. The banks host the bustling downtown, with its bazaars, restaurants, and coffee shops. Some of the oldest streets in the city, Al-Rasheed and Al-Nahar, lead to the popular shopping districts, Souq Daniel, Souq al-Arabi, and Souq al-Ghazal (the pet bazaar). The area is a mix of cultures and religions, with mosques and churches situated meters away from each other. The smell of lamb tikka and skewers of beef liver grilling on glowing coal fires entices the passersby, distracting them from their destinations to stop for a quick morning snack. Vendors steep chai with cardamom, sweet and dark, in porcelain teapots for workers, shop owners, and peddlers alike. There is something in the air that is energetic and indolent all at once, and there is an abiding sense of being and belonging here.

The Zahawi Café

On the corner of Al-Rasheed Street,
the coffee shop rests
under its faded sign of painted
whitewashed wood;
its shutters open to
exhausted cab horns, clattering hoofs,
cracked voices of boy peddlers shuffling
in oversized shoes;
their eyes darting toward the
light dancing on the languid river.
Inside, fans sigh,
dice skip over striped wooden boards,
and the cheers of the men get stopped by the
screech of table legs against tile floors.
The walls are adorned with the solemn faces
of kings and poets,
now fogged by smoke
streaming from hand-wrapped cigarettes,
wedged between brown rheumatic fingers,
that strike notes with spoons against
glasses of chai on small plates,
speckled with crystals of sugar.
Silver heads wrapped
with black and white kafiyas,
nod to stories flowing from quivering lips,
tales that blend with the scents
and the hum
and drown
in the swirls of
the silent river.

Situated in the middle of the ever-evolving city around it, an early thirteenth-century school, Al-Madrasah al-Mustansiriya, was one of the first universities in the world. At one time, it boasted thousands of books in its library and offered education to seekers from all over the world. The area is a mixture of old and new, with streets like Souq al-Sifafeer and Shari' al-Mutanabbi that have been part of Baghdadi culture for centuries. The former is filled with shops selling ornaments of copper; inside the covered market, craftsmen hammer away at shiny copper trays, dillal (coffee pots), and all sizes of makahil (kohl pots). Close by is Al-Mutanabbi Street—the street of the booksellers. Books on religion and politics, philosophy and history, as well as school texts, novels, and children's books—all varieties of literature— can be found displayed on the sidewalks.

Al-Mutanabbi Street

When I was fifteen, I used to visit Al-Mutanabbi Street with my mother. Literature from around the world was carefully stacked along the sidewalks, young and old people reading, browsing, haggling for that perfect price. The tiny overstocked shops had barely enough room to walk between the towers of books. Shy and awkward, I would follow my mother through the wood and glass doorways.

The smell of dust and old, yellow paper was intoxicating. She would ask for books in English. "Upstairs," the storeowner would say and point us toward a narrow wooden staircase that led to a windowless room housing all the foreign-language books. I would climb up, my eyes seeking out titles on the shelves before I had even reached the final step, under the single dust-coated light bulb struggling to shine. My mom would pull out a crate and sit down.

"Go ahead, take your time," she would say and wave her hand at me. She knew that books had become my refuge in Baghdad, and she would sit patiently while I flipped through them carefully, trying desperately not to inhale the dark dust that covered everything around me. Time raced as I pulled book after book from the shelves, until something would catch my eye.

One time it was a grey book cover, small and rough. *Romeo and Juliet*. I opened the yellowed pages, smelt the paper, and handed it to my mom. Then I handed her another one.

"Another Shakespeare?" She stared at me.

Complete works, signed on the first page, a gift for someone. Beautiful penmanship, no cover.

"Why not find something that has a cover?"

Another time it was J R R Tolkien's *The Hobbit* and T H White's *The Once and Future King* under a film of fine dust. I carefully removed them from the shelves, turned them sideways, and watched the dust slide off into a pile on the floor. I added them to my small library in my bedroom. Later, I began reading Stephen King novels; I would stay up all night engrossed in their sordid details and get startled by the slightest sounds outside the glass doors of my balcony.

When I became more confident with my Arabic, I began to read works by the Egyptian writers Taha Hussein and Ihsan Abdel Quddous and the Syrian poet Nizzar Qabbani. They introduced me to the nuances of Arab culture and history; Qabbani also gave me more modern perspectives on love and female power. From Qabbani I moved on to the pre-Islamic poets and the Muallaqat—the Hanging Poems, which used to hang inside the Kaaba in Mecca. I had been introduced to them in high school and was required to memorize them. At first the language had baffled me and sounded like gibberish. Then as I read through the works of Imru' al-Qais, I discovered the richness of the poems and the depth of meaning they held.

My love for reading grew, but my access to diverse authors and topics was limited. Once, one of my schoolfriends lent me Alix Kate Shulman's *Burning Questions*, which confused and shocked me. I hid the book between my geometry and biology homework, and would read it while my parents were out. I would place it under my mattress when I left the house to hide it from my mother, who had a tendency to flip through my work from time to time. For some fleeting moments, I felt rebellious and daring.

It would not be until many years later, when I was thousands of kilometers away from those shops, that I would understand how limited my access to books had been.

After the American invasion of 2003, the bookstores began keeping more contemporary American titles. American soldiers would sell their books to the shops, which became flooded with stacks of cheap romance and crime novels. The British classics were relegated to the corners for English Literature students and connoisseurs. Traces of the early twentieth-century British Mandate began to be replaced with the neo-imperialist American presence. American occupation was not just a physical presence; it crawled into every aspect of our lifestyles.

On March 5 2007, a car bomb exploded in Al-Mutanabbi Street, killing or injuring dozens of vendors and shoppers. This was one of many attacks aimed to cripple the intellectual factions of Iraqi society. From the kidnappings of school children for ransom to the executions of Iraq's most well-known professionals and academics, the country witnessed the draining of its brightest minds.

Becoming Iraqi

In the years following the first Gulf War, I began to appreciate and embrace my Iraqi identity. I understood the ways of our society, what it viewed as inappropriate and what was required from me as a young woman. As I grew out of my teenage years, I learned how to adapt to the culture. I began to love my country and understand the pressures that the war had brought to a tired and struggling people. Iraqis are proud and resilient, but fun-loving too. We are a generous people;

even those with very little means open their homes to visitors and share their meals without hesitation. They have a long Arab tradition of generosity, courtesy, and hospitality. Most homes did not have phones, so our extended family and friends would show up any time at our door for a visit, without prior notice. As soon as they arrived, my mother would begin to prepare a meal and provide space and bedding for naps or overnight stays. While it was not always convenient, hospitality was a fundamental part of our culture.

After I finished high school, my parents bought and renovated a house in the Al-Harthia neighborhood. They put all their money and their dreams into that home: white stone columns, grey marble floors, a spiraling staircase, and many details that they argued over constantly during the renovations. When the house was complete, it was always filled with our friends, neighbors, and members of our extended family.

My cousins were my closest friends; they taught me how to enjoy living in Iraq and find ways around the limitations of a patriarchal society. The young women around me dressed in the latest fashions, most learned to drive at sixteen, and they found their own ways to express their freedom in a conservative society. Every Tuesday, Shayma and I would go for swimming and lunch at the Hunting Club with my cousin Ghsoun and a group of friends. There we lost all sense of etiquette and giggled uncontrollably over gossip and jokes, oblivious of stares from other patrons. Sometimes we gathered for potlucks and lavish sixties- and seventies-themed birthday and Halloween parties. Other times my friends and I skipped classes and visited fortunetellers to have our fortunes read from the grounds of Turkish coffee in little cups.

My cousins and friends are now spread out in many different countries: Iraq, Jordan, England, Sweden, Germany, the United Arab Emirates, Canada, and the United States.

Photographs

I turn the stiff, rough pages
inhale every detail.

My fingers trace the
sage, sapphire, and crimson
of Kashmir carpets
spread under our feet.

They trace the
hollows and mounds of
Seven Eyes,
cobalt and shiny,
hanging
above solid oak doorways,
forbidding evil spirits,
evil eyes,
and djinn.

I glimpse
our fingers entwined,
bodies in concert
as feet rise and fall
to the rhythm of chobbi,
and the twirl of misbaha beads.

Those glossy prints
full of
blushed laughter
that floats on the surface
beckon sensations
release spiraling streams
of incense,

that hover
for days.

We are motionless,
forever in that space,
in those moments,
in which we were
the happiest.

Our lives were far different from the stereotypical images portrayed in the West. The concepts of agency for women in Iraq are much more complex than the simplistic interpretations of Western scholars and media. Iraqi women studied in schools and colleges, held high positions in private and public professions, raised families, and actively participated in building their communities. They held together their households during the wars, ran businesses, and kept government bureaucracies running when the men were fighting wars. We were by no means imprisoned in our homes and prohibited from further education, nor were we oppressed by our fathers, brothers, and husbands. Our cultural norms simply differed from those of the West, which we never needed to uphold in the first place.

—

I finished high school. Most Iraqi students aimed for medicine, engineering, or the sciences and became very competitive in their senior years. They would prepare for the final year throughout the summer, with the help of tutors, additional classes, and study groups, and drowned themselves in stress. I never aimed for anything in particular and my marks were low compared to those of my peers. My parents felt that I had failed to reach my potential. Through the centralized university admission process, I was placed in a program to train as a dental hygienist, but my father decided that I should apply to the English department at a private teaching college in Baghdad.

"You read all the time; an English department would be a good choice for you," Baba said.

"I don't know if that's what I want to do, Baba," I replied, my eyes downcast. I was upset that I had not worked harder, but I still had not decided what my path should be.

"You don't have many options. At least you will use one of your strengths to develop teaching skills. Maybe you'll become a high school teacher." He ended the conversation. A few weeks later we visited the Assistant Dean of Al-Moman University College and I applied to their English program.

After the first week there, I began to enjoy studying the history of English literature and analyzing literary texts. I was like a sponge. I wanted to learn everything in those courses and my grades reflected my enthusiasm. After graduation, my parents encouraged me to complete a master's degree at the College of Arts at the University of Baghdad, one of the oldest English departments in Iraq. While my cousins and classmates began to think about marriage, I was meeting with department heads to ask about their graduate programs. My father felt that my degrees were more important than marriage.

"At least finish your master's degree; it will open opportunities for you wherever you end up. Marriage will come when it's destined," he said.

FIVE

Baghdad, March 2003

Mine was a "semitraditional" Iraqi marriage. Esam's friends knew my friends and we met briefly before he sent his parents to ask for my hand in marriage. In the eight-month period between our first meeting and the actual engagement ceremony, we had the opportunity to get to know each other.

> I remember the day he came to the university to see me for the
>   first time.
> I was dressed in mourning for my aunt Buthayna:
> head to toe in black,
> my hair pulled back,
> no makeup,
> only a line of kohl colored my eyelids.
> We didn't speak.
> I saw his shoes first,
> I don't remember seeing his face that day.
>
> But I remember the day they introduced us very clearly.
> Standing in front of my mirror before we met,

still in mourning,
quietly praying that Allah would choose the right one for me,
I asked Him to give me a sign.
I remember that knot in my stomach
as we entered the living room
with our friends, who had set up the meeting.
I remember his eyes,
how they reflected shades of green
under his glasses.
His voice was strong.
He commanded attention when he spoke
and something about him made me feel safe.

Untraditionally,
we met in the courtyards
of the University, Bab al-Muadum,
sitting on sun-scalded benches.
One day during Ramadan,
we broke our fast with our families
in the upstairs restaurant of the Hunting Club.
In those months before the official engagement,
we fell in love.

For eight months, his family came to visit my parents,
insisted we proceed with the ceremonies.
It was late February 2002, when my father gave his consent.

We exchanged our engagement rings in front of our families.
Despite the announcement of our intent to marry, there were still
restrictions: we were not yet married in the eyes of God nor was the
union approved by a magistrate. In March, we went before a magistrate and received our official marriage contract. This ceremony, one
of many before the actual wedding, gave us more liberty to meet with

each other and go out, sometimes by yourselves, to finish up furnishing and preparing our house.

Esam traveled with me and my family to Kurdistan in northern Iraq, where we celebrated Nawrooz with Kurdish families dancing on the edges of Duhok: the women in bright shimmering dresses and the men in their traditional sharweel pants. Esam and I had our first fight among the ancient city ruins of Al-Hadr, under the watchful eyes of Shahiro. In a photograph from that trip taken just after our fight, I am sitting, my back to a white stone wall, my eyebrows knitted against the bright sunlight, glaring at him as he takes the picture on his digital camera.

Out of the many wedding ceremonies that we have in Iraq, my favorites are Aqad al-Quran—a religious ceremony—and Al-Henna—a kind of farewell for the bride. We had decided to combine the two ceremonies into a single celebration. The night before my wedding, my parents' home was filled with women—aunts, cousins, friends, and neighbors gathered in our family living room dressed in colorful gallabiyas decorated with beads. I sat quietly in my white, chiffon gallabiya, its edges hand-painted in gold and silver by Khala Hanna. Standing on either side, two of my cousins held a long cloth over my head, while another cousin rubbed blocks of sugar over the cloth. I could not move, I had to stay still, my feet immersed in a glass bowl of water infused with magnolia and jasmine, cardamom pods tightly pressed between my fingers. Smells of henna and various herbs and spices wafted up from a tray placed next to me; earlier that day, each spice and herb had been carefully selected by the spice merchant and sorted by my cousins to ensure good fortune, happiness, and a successful marital bond. The flame from a three-foot candle, decorated with ribbons and flowers, flickered and settled as the ceremony began.

Apart from my reading from the Quran in my lap, the rituals were less religious and more traditional. I looked away from the mirror, held up in front of my face, and the stares from the women anticipating my "yes" to the Sayyed, who was performing the ceremony from the other side of the living-room door. I could not focus on a line and kept glossing over the page, my mind straying to Esam, soon to be my husband, in the other room. I waited for the Sayyed to finish his questions.

"Do you agree to marry this man?" The bearded old man's voice drifted through the crack in the door.

"Yes," I said firmly. He had to hear it clearly.

The room hushed into a momentary silence.

Then, like ringing bells, ululations filled the house.

We were married in May without the extravagant wedding celebrations that my cousins and friends had had. My seamstress had sewn my wedding dress from a lightly beaded lace and organza fabric that I had found hidden under rolls of fabric in a tiny shop in Al-Kadumia market, and one of my mother's friends added some more beads and a veil. It was simple and light.

We went on our honeymoon to Damascus and Amman. It was my first time out of the country since I was thirteen, and my first time completely alone with my husband.

Baghdad, March 10 2003

The first thought that entered my mind as I held Ameen was that it was a waste of time to love any man because my true love lay sleeping in my arms. Born three weeks early, my baby saved me the hassle of a birth in the middle of the war. All the midwives we had contacted, all the medicines we had gathered—our preparations for an emergency home birth during the invasion—were put aside and I was allowed the decency of a "normal," natural childbirth under the supervision of doctors and nurses.

But the pregnancy and delivery were a nightmare. Apart from the constant apprehension of an upcoming invasion, the actual experience of giving birth, when the time came, was terrifying. I had heard that hospital staff and nurses could be aggressive. I was three weeks early when I felt the first hints of pain and discomfort after a night out for dinner and a walk with friends. One of them, sitting across from me at dinner, had said, "You look like you might have the baby tonight."

"Why do you say that?" I laughed nervously.

"I don't know, there is an expression on your face that's similar to my sister's when she went into labor," she replied with a smile.

That night, I could not sleep. The gradually intensifying pain kept me restless; I walked around the house, took a shower, and finally woke my husband up after midnight. We called my mother to meet us at the hospital. I was in one of the best hospitals in Baghdad and my family knew most of the doctors there, but giving birth in Iraq was not an experience that we had eagerly anticipated. My friends and cousins who had given birth before me had hated everything about it; some of them had been constantly berated by the staff for their anxieties and for expressing their pain openly during childbirth. We had little or no access to epidural anesthesia, so apart from cesareans all our births were natural. I had asked my family to arrange a home birth for me because the traditional midwives were known to be more empathetic, but they were hesitant because it was my first child. And my husband wanted to make sure that everything went smoothly.

After forty-eight hours of labor, the nurses and doctors who had gently cared for me had to change shifts. When the pain escalated and I let out a low scream, a young female resident doctor came into my room and yelled at me to calm down. But this did not stop me from screaming at the top of my lungs at the next contraction. I sometimes try to explain that feeling to others: it is like a hand that reaches into your chest and pulls out your soul. I pursed my lips tightly to suppress the scream, but with the following contraction it rang through the hospital halls and outside to the parking lot (as one of my acquaintances claims). At some point my exclamations of pain came out in English, and I yelled out, "Oh God!"

A nurse shouted, "Say 'Ya Allah' instead!"

She bent down and said into my ear, "Stop screaming now! You are making a scene! What is all this nonsense?"

I went quiet for a second, then I pulled myself up by the two side handles of the bed, looked her straight in the eye, and said, "Enough! I will curse you if you ask me to stop screaming again!" People believed that a woman's wishes and curses expressed during labor came true.

Her face lost color and she pleaded, "No, don't say that please! I am just asking you to calm down."

From then onward, she did not say anything to me except "Push!"

———

I went back home that same day and felt as if this were my only purpose in life. I was born to be a mother. God had sent me a child to keep my mind off the coming days. I did not care if America was going to attack, I did not care that my husband was preparing our home for bombings and chemical weapons. All I cared about was changing diapers and feeding this little being that needed my utmost attention.

My family came for visits to see Ameen, my father even stole away from work to stand over his precious first grandchild and smiled proudly. I did not want to think past those days, those moments.

From My Diary

March 18 2003

A beautiful baby boy. I gave birth at 8:55 Monday morning on the 10th of March. I went through a hell of a labor that lasted for three days! [. . .] I saw his head and it was like time stopped for a few seconds and when they brought him [to me] it was like a dream.

I haven't written because with all the baby's needs we're waiting for war in 2 days.

March 2003

I watched Esam tape the windows and cover every possible opening around the house with plastic sheets. I saw him prepare kerosene
and gas for cooking and fuel for the car in case we needed to flee.
I shut everything out. But as the days moved along and the tension
rose around us, my family decided that the only way to help me care
for the baby was for them to come and stay with me. Ten days passed
and the war was upon us. We had secretly installed a satellite dish on
the roof and we all huddled upon my bed, waiting, watching the Iraqi
army in the streets.

My parents and Shayma slept in the nursery, which was across from
our room. Haydar and his new bride, Sara, slept under the staircase in
the hallway. Although we had a large home, we all felt a need to stay
as close as we could to each other for safety and comfort. The uncertainty ate at our senses and the months of build-up had left everyone anxious. I think, secretly, we just wanted everything to begin so it
could finally end.

The first missiles hit while we were having dinner in our kitchen.
The sound of sirens filled the house and I felt my heart lurch inside
me. We quickly left the table and ran toward the safety of the bed-
rooms. Sara ducked to the ground, shaking with fear. She was with
a new family, far from her own parents and brothers. I gave her my
hand, helped her get up, and pulled her toward the hallway.

With all our previous experiences of war and missile attacks, we
should have been prepared for that sound. As I write about those
moments, my heart races and I become breathless. The feeling, I think,
is helplessness and loss of control over our very existence.

Missiles

As the sound of missiles tore through the sky, the man I was married
to was still very much a stranger to me; we still had not completed a

year of marriage. We would grow closer day by day as we embarked on the most difficult time of our lives together. Our patience, our marriage, and our immature love would be tested by a war that would change all our plans and dreams.

One of my very first childhood memories is of sirens screaming during the air raids in the Iran-Iraq War. At the time we were living in the southern city of Basra. When the sirens sounded, I would hide under the stairs with my mother, my head buried in her lap. A long, winding scream would ring in my ears. I could sense the fear in my mother's shivering body and the deep, broken breaths she struggled to take. I did not know what was happening, but I understood that I had to obey her whispers to, "Sit and stay still!"

I remember my fear of the darkness that enveloped the house and the silence in my head.

Fear grows
with the rising sound
of the missile;
as the roar grows,
a black hole forms
inside the body
and swells,
drowning all the senses.
That sound is distinct,
so much an urgent scream.
The missile is personal,
intended only for you.
Although it may not find you,
it lives forever inside you.
Fear is strange at these times.
It is not the fear of death.
It is the fear of being
one of the bodies in that flash on the screen.

Mangled and torn,

anonymous,

eyes open to the skies.

Predictions of War

A couple of months before the invasion, we had sat around the kitchen table in my parents' home in Al-Harthia. My swollen belly pushed into the edge of the table each time I reached out for something to put on my plate from the meal that Mother had made. I had taken a shower and my hair was still wet, loosely wrapped in a towel. I was totally relaxed and comfortable.

Haydar, Sara, and my parents were discussing the growing threat of another American invasion.

"It'll be like the first one."

"A few weeks and we will be back to normal."

"We just have to get through those weeks."

I had heard numerous speculations, fears, and horrific rumors about the coming invasion. A few weeks before, my husband and I had seen Ridley Scott's *Black Hawk Down*. The movie left us with an unpleasant taste in our mouths. We had watched the "heroic" Americans infiltrating foreign government buildings, saving lives, saving a country, all in just over two hours. The American perspective of the world, we thought, was limited and far from reality. The idea in these films is always to make the Americans themselves feel good: about themselves, about their young men fighting American-invented battles overseas, about killing and destroying nations and populations they have never known or understood.

———

I was four months pregnant, visiting the English department at the University of Baghdad, when one of my professors asked me if I would stay to meet an American journalist. He led me to his office where a young faculty member was waiting with the journalist.

The journalist was aggressively condescending. I watched intently his smug face, his partly bald head somewhat sunburned and sweaty as he repeatedly adjusted his glasses on the ridge of his nose.

"What do you think will happen?" he asked.

"I think Iraqis will defend their country," I replied, stating what I believed but also very conscious that my answers must show my patriotic side to the others in the room.

"Don't you think that they will turn against each other?"

The professor, who was seated in the corner of the room behind the journalist, looked at me and replied before I could answer, "We have a saying: Me and my cousin against the enemy, me and my brother against my cousin."

"Why do you think they will rise against the American troops?" the journalist asked with a smirk.

"Would you want a burglar in your home. Wouldn't you defend it?" I asked sharply. My hand was beginning to shake on the table, and I placed it quietly in my lap.

He looked into my eyes and answered in a very serious voice.

"We will meet in six months and see if that happens. Of course, if this building is still standing," he concluded sarcastically.

He was threatening me, a young pregnant woman, whom he had never met before. He was threatening my people's lives and smiling. Sitting in the corner of the room, the professor raised his eyebrows, signaling to me and my colleague to end the conversation.

Al-Suwayrah, March 2003

A couple of days after the first airstrike, we fled from Baghdad to Esam's hometown, Al-Suwayrah, about an hour away. After the constant air raids we had suffered, we feared that we would be unable to leave Baghdad if the situation became worse. The city felt like it was constantly exploding around us. With the sirens, the mosques around Baghdad would call for prayer, "Allahu Akbar, Allahu Akbar. La Illaha Ila Allah," and this would be followed by the sound of church bells ringing, as if answering the call. The intention was to raise the morale of the people in their neighborhoods. But in reality, they seemed to emphasize our inability to do anything except pray. The hair on my arms would rise every time the call for prayer began; in a chain of calls, each neighborhood passed on the message of forthcoming doom.

We knew that the Americans intended to erase us; if they had wanted to remove Saddam Hussein, there were less violent ways of taking him out. No one was safe. In the first Gulf War, they had bombed Al-Amiriyah Shelter, which had housed hundreds of civilians, mostly women and children. Fathers and husbands had dropped off their families there, hoping they would have a better chance of surviving the air raids. Four hundred and eight civilians died that night. The three missiles that hit the shelter led to the doors locking from impact and imprisoning people within the burning walls. I had seen images of the shelter and went to the annual memoriam at the site; the remains of bodies were plastered on the walls of the shelter.

Shock and Awe, as George W Bush called it, was exactly that. Everything was a target: we saw smoke rising from different parts of the city, until the smoke was all we could see.

Esam hired a driver with a big Dyna truck and we emptied the freezer and the fridge, packed canned foods and medical supplies. He went through the house checking doors and windows, making sure they were all taped to prevent them from shattering during the bombings. I watched as he moved around from room to room, thinking that we might not find these rooms when we returned. I cherished that house and the memories we had created in it. I quietly walked behind him reciting prayers, asking for God's grace and mercy, "La asaluka rad alkadhaa, asaluka al lutfah feh."

I went into Ameen's nursery, went through the custom-made pine bedroom set my parents had made for him. He had not even had the chance to sleep in the crib because we still kept him in a Moses basket next to my bedside. His wardrobe was filled with the clothes we had gathered from shops in Al-Mansour and Al-Karrada, which still did not fit because he was so small. I began packing them, and took down the hand-made quilt and the cross-stitched butterfly, both of which I had made for him during my pregnancy. I felt lost and overwhelmed.

In the postpartum period, by tradition an Iraqi mother goes back to her family home to recover and be cared for. For forty days she is taught to take care of her newborn by the older women of the family; her mother, sisters, aunts, and cousins dote over her and her child before she goes back to her husband's home to resume her responsibilities. I had not been able to go to my parents' house because of fear of the impending attack. They lived close to the government buildings and presidential palaces, which were potential targets. Unlike other new mothers, I was on my feet, cleaning, cooking, and bracing myself for the inevitable unknown. Now, I was being forced out of the comfort of my beloved home. I felt cheated out of my right to rest and experience motherhood, but in those rushed moments, as we hastily left, I had no time to stop and lament the loss.

As a government employee, my father was back in military uniform, even though he had been a civilian since the beginning of the Iran-Iraq War. His job as an animal science researcher kept him far from combat, but he was still required to be on call for military duty if needed to defend his country. Since he was moved around to different locations around Baghdad, he decided that my mother, Shayma, Haydar, and Sara should leave Baghdad with us, hoping that Al-Suwayrah would be safer.

The Road to Al-Suwayrah

The road to Al-Suwayrah was crowded with fleeing cars and units of the Iraqi army. The soldiers were burning crude oil on the sides of the road in order to mislead American jets. There is an Arabic saying that roughly translates, "There is misfortune that is comical"—comical in the sense that it is so tragic, so incomprehensible that you can do nothing but laugh at it. But I find that, even in the safety of my home here in Canada years later, I am unable to laugh at that scene.

As the black smoke coiled around us, my husband railed against their stupidity, while I held an oversized mask to my newborn's face, trying desperately to prevent the smoke from entering his lungs. I feared that we would die at the hands of our own people.

Comical.

The soldiers were laughing, perhaps thinking that their tactics would work against an army that did not need to see their targets.

Comical.

The chaos on the road was simply overwhelming. The usually empty fields around us overflowed with soldiers, heavy artillery, and tanks. We began to regret our decision to leave Baghdad.

We arrived in Al-Suwayrah emotionally and physically exhausted.

———

Al-Suwayrah is a small town less than an hour's drive south of Baghdad. Esam's family lands and orchards are situated on the banks of the Tigris—Dijla—at the edge of that town. In the middle of a lovely orchard, his father, Ammo Atta, had built a beautiful house, with high windows that looked out to the river, with the hope that it would be a retreat from the city during the holidays. After Esam's mother passed away in 1989, however, the house was rarely used. Even after his father remarried, the only time the family had actually stayed there was to escape the first Gulf War in 1991.

Esam's uncle, Ammo Hassouni, and his family lived down the street from there. After some discussion, and some exhortation from Ammo

Hassouni's family to stay with them, we decided that Esam, Ameen, and I would stay at Esam's uncle's home and my mother, Haydar, Sara and Shayma would move to his father's.

Ammo Hassouni had settled on his family's land, surrounded by the homes of cousins and relatives. Their orchards had rows of date palms and citrus and fruit trees. I had been here several times before and greatly enjoyed myself. During our summer visits our hosts would fill our car with crates of pomegranates, small white apples, black and

green figs, sweet apricots, loquat, and persimmons.

However, as an in-law, I was still a stranger in Ammo Hassouni's family and felt comforted that my own family was a few doors down the street. It was expected that the American invasion would come over land, and my brother felt that the responsibility of protecting three women, his mother, wife, and sister, in a new neighborhood was too much. He hardly slept, preferring to stay awake to guard the house. After a few days, he decided to take them back to Baghdad.

His decision terrified me, but I knew that the responsibility would be too much to bear for him if they were actually attacked. I remained quiet and watched them drive back to Baghdad, not knowing when or if I would see them again.

With the phone lines cut, we had no way of reaching them, until one day my parents surprised us, arriving at the gate of Ammo Hassouni's house. They had driven through the roads and fields filled with Iraqi army units in order to check on us.

> I wanted to cry, to tell them
> to take me back with them.
> I didn't want to be wife and mother.
> I was not ready for this new role.
> But always smiling,
> I served them tea and chatted,
> brought them their grandson
> to hold,
> until they had to leave.
> They watched my face,
> with worry and longing.
> I stood at the gate,
> the comfort of their presence
> drained from my body.
> I turned to smile at my husband,
> as I walked toward the bedroom.
> Closing the door tightly after me,
> I cried
> quietly,
> desperately trying to stifle
> my sobs in the palms of my hands,
> wishing my mother still had her arms
> around me.

Al-Suwayrah 2003

Ameen cried for hours from a rash that moved down his thigh.

"It's the water," they said, "it's contaminated."

Mechanically, I changed and bathed him.

"I don't want to be a mother now," I thought.

What would I tell him of his first days? That I was lost like the millions around me? At night, I would turn my back to him and silently cry till I fell asleep. If an air raid began, I would not hold him, fearing that I would suffocate him if I held him too tight. So many nights I worried that my husband and I would not survive those air raids, and Ameen would be alone. I imagined him crying, no one to care for him or hold him.

I could feel his little heart under the fragile bones of his ribcage, so persistent, so unaware of everything around him.

———

When Esam's parents decided to leave Baghdad and join us in Al-Suwayrah, we moved from Ammo Hassouni's home to Ammo Atta's house, to join Esam's family—his father, stepmother, Nadia, and brothers, Taha and Wissam. We did not know how long we would stay there.

Once again, the old routine of war set in. This time I was surrounded by my new family, and I busied myself with the baby and the chores. Diapers were hard to find and expensive when available. Ameen was so small that he would get lost in store-bought diapers; they were limited to one size, large, which was too big for a newborn, covering the body up to the neck. And so I had to use small, square white cloths, which meant that I had to wash piles of them daily. My hands would get raw and bloody from the scrubbing to make those diapers white.

We had no clean running water, except from a single tap at the edge of the patio, and no electricity, except from a small generator we had brought with us. Once in a while, Esam would turn on the generator to help me with washing the baby's clothes in a small single-tub washer. We depended mostly on candles and kerosene lamps, using the generator fuel for sporadically watching news on television and doing laundry.

———

During daytime, the sounds of the missiles were more bearable and jets breaking the sound barrier could be easily ignored. The attacks at night were another story. One night the air raids sounded very close to the house. We could hear missiles screaming and the loud explosions that followed. Fearing that the windows would shatter from the blasts, we decided to sit outside on the porch. My mother-in-law, a small, frail woman, brought out a blanket and pulled it over our heads, then she put an arm around me and Ameen to keep us warm on the steps of the concrete porch. Her whole body trembled; I could hear her teeth rattling as she tried desperately to read Suwrat al-Fateha and Ayet al-Kursi from the Quran. She would pause with every explosion and begin again, "Bismallah al-rahman al-rahim" (In the name of God, the most gracious, the most merciful). The attack seemed to last for hours. The next day we heard that a weapons storage facility had been attacked, which explained the successive blasts that had lit up the night skies.

A couple of days later, in another air raid, one of the neighboring orchards was hit. Forty date palms had been blown into the Dijla, leaving a gaping crater in their place.

———

On television we watched as our beloved Baghdad was destroyed. The screen was our only connection to the devastation taking place less than an hour away. We felt helpless, angry, and defeated. How was it possible that the world watched quietly as we were being systematically erased?

In those images on the screen, I would search for my father. I remembered the names of the neighborhoods in which he would be stationed. All of those locations had been bombed. I anxiously watched the images of the dead flash quickly on the screen, praying that I saw no one familiar. The cameras moved over the fallen bodies, all twisted in unnatural ways. I would turn toward Esam.

"No, your father is not there," he would reply immediately, "he's been moved somewhere else." He refused to indulge my fears any further, always abruptly ending our conversations on the matter. But the images of bodies in official clothes began to pile up on our screen. I would leave the living room and curl up on my bed, crying until Ameen cried out for attention.

———

During the invasion, I ran to Dijla for safety.
We hid under the orange and lemon trees
on her banks,
but they found us
anyway.
With their cluster bombs,
they shredded the orchards around our home;
they uprooted our memories,
our childhood.
I could hear the drones
float over the roof
buzzing like gigantic insects
from some sci-fi movie,
sucking our lives through their lenses.
I had thought only God
could watch us from above.

We would sit
closely huddled together:
the men guessing
which places were being attacked,
the women praying
through clenched teeth.
The nights were dark
and we walked blind,
through hallways
that caved in around us.

———

One day we heard the men urgently whispering to each other. They were restless, opening doors and closing them, going in and out of the darkness outside the ring of candlelight.

"They're coming,"

"I can hear the tanks."

"What will we do with the women?"

Who was coming? The candlelight made masks of their faces. People were outside the orchard gates.

"You have to leave!" our men said to them. "We have families inside and a baby. These are civilian homes."

The Iraqi army we had seen stationed in the fields along the road to Al-Suwayrah could no longer stay in the open. They needed the thick vegetation of the orchards for camouflage.

"We have nowhere else to go; we need to hide under the trees, *they are coming closer!*" The soldiers pleaded, but eventually they left.

Later we found mutilated tanks on the road leading to the orchard. There were no bodies, only scrunched metal and bullet casings scattered on the earth.

I feel guilty to this day.

My Ghosts Return

My ghosts have returned
from the ditches
of the Western Desert,
from the waters of the Tigris
they stand dripping soot
beside my bed
waiting
for relief,
for recognition.

I pass through them
at the iron gate.
They tug at the strands
of my hair,
they touch my face
with cold fingers,
smiling.

I find sand on my Persian rugs
and muddy footsteps on the
wooden floors.

They smile and tease
They ask to enter...re-enter;
they have never left,
have been always here
by the night light
on my bedside table,
lulling me to sleep
with melodies

singing, "Your enemy lies wounded on the desert sands."[11]

My enemy lies in me,
pulling at the oud strings,
knowing I will let them in,
knowing they have
never
left
my side.

Suwayrah 2003

Lying on our bed soaked with sweat and the damp that covers the house, I hear a whistle, like the call of a bird. I move closer to the body next to mine.

"I think they are coming from the river."

He sits up in bed, trying to discern the sounds.

What is it? Something is approaching the window in front of our bed. Images from American war movies reel in my head. I keep imagining their faces striped green and black, their helmets strung with leaves as they creep out of the river and into our backyard.

They will be here any minute. They will take us, our land, our bodies, our sanity.

In that moment of terror, I recalled overhearing one of my uncles saying once during the first Gulf War, "If the American troops attack the house, I will kill all the women in the family and then myself!"

The Soldiers Come

under the stairs
in the dark hallway
we hide you and I

---

11 The line is a loose translation from a traditional Iraqi lullaby.

I hear their footsteps
by the rusting gate
they come closer
come closer my child
my body wants to
surround you
to inhale you
to bury you
in its flesh
to crush you
within its folds
to make you disappear
crushed together
longing for walls
to absorb our bodies
pressing back
till the paint seems
to crawl into
the pores of our skin

maybe they won't see us
hiding in the shadows
under the stairs
their whispers are clear now

hush don't cry
your tears fall
like boulders from cliffs
on glass
they shatter the stillness
they dent my brain
they stream down your cheeks
taking my youth, taking my years

my youth is now lost
in the strands of white and grey
in the cold marble floor
as we crouch under the stairs
you and I
we wait.

The Fall

We never imagined the speed with which the Americans would enter Baghdad. Iraqi officials always denied American progress. Al-Sahaf, the Information Minister, would appear on the screen, which became our entire world, and lie to us, saying that the Iraqi army was still in control.

"The Americans are far from Baghdad. We are victorious," he would claim repeatedly, while CNN's cameras showed the tanks parading along Saddam Airport Highway, the familiar street signs and buildings passing swiftly before us. And then finally, the propaganda leaflets began to rain down on us from the skies, telling us to surrender peacefully. People were afraid to pick them up. We feared accusations of treason and avoided them or discreetly discarded them. Confused and in denial, we wanted desperately to believe that Baghdad was still holding out against the American invasion.

On the television, I saw an American tank on a bridge near our home in Zayouna. I turned to Esam and shouted that they were in our neighborhood. He said no, all the bridges looked the same. He looked at his brother, whose face was as expressionless. Of course, he had only been trying to shield me from the terrible reality. Now, as the American tanks rolled all over Baghdad, he could not hide the magnitude of what was taking place any longer.

Reality had suddenly become a very abstract construct; we had become dislocated from it, as though living in some Hollywood war film. I watched the fall of our nation displayed on the television screen, while I sat folding my son's clothes on a couch by the stairs.

> We woke up on the ninth of April and watched the statue in
>   the square fall;
> watched marines climb up the statue and cover Saddam's head
>   with their red, white and blue;
> watched Iraqis jeering and the flag replaced with an Iraqi one;
> watched Iraqi men hit the bronze face of the dictator with san-
>   dals and shoes,
> watched the chaos screaming at us from the screen, filling us
>   with confusion, fear, and anger.
> And we knew this was it.

There was nothing we could do except sit there together in disbelief. We had so little time to digest the extent of what had taken place that day. We had remained silent, watching, hoping that it was all a show, a way to weaken the Iraqi spirit. I think that all we managed to utter, as we watched, were indistinct exclamations of disbelief. I kept telling myself that the Iraqi army would appear soon and take back the city. But all the illusions of the past months that the Iraqi government had tried to build, of a proud, powerful, and united people and government, had been shattered on that television screen. We would never be saved from the invading forces; we were now an occupied nation under merciless military control.

Growing up under the rule of Saddam Hussein was not easy; even his own family members were not safe. He killed his sons-in-law and his brother-in-law, and attempted to kill his own son when he felt threatened. But what really broke the Iraqi people were the wars. Generation after generation, the Iraqis lost loved ones to the senseless wars with Iran and the United States. They endured sanctions and financial instability. They spent years unable to leave the country due to restrictions on travel, effectively imprisoned within the borders of their own country. Saddam Hussein's rule was brutal and we had lived in constant fear of government officials and the Mukhabarat— the Iraqi Intelligence Agency—but the foreign occupation was more demeaning and more frightening. Under the false banner of liberation, a foreign power now had ultimate control over the lives and future of my people. The Americans were not the saviors; they too had their own agendas and their sense of entitlement to our resources. Iraqi people were the collateral damage in both situations.

I had grown up reading and listening to inspiring stories about people fighting for their freedom from foreign rule. In school we had covered the histories of rebellions and revolutions from all around the Arab world. The persistence of Arab revolutionaries from Algeria to Palestine filled us with a will to resist any form of occupation. Now I watched some Iraqis accepting and supporting the American invasion, falling for the monotonous preaching of democracy by American news networks. They believed they were being liberated from a tyrant, unaware of the greater horrors that the American invasion and occupation would bring.

The Road to Baghdad

After watching the chaos portrayed on the news, Esam and his brother, Taha, decided that we should head back to Baghdad to secure our homes from looting and vandalism, which was rampant all over the city.

I do not think anything would have prepared us for the scenes that unfolded as we drove toward Baghdad. We maneuvered our car through a sea of destroyed Iraqi tanks. The road was like a maze, covered with bullet casings, mangled pieces of metal, and the carcasses of dead animals. I kept averting my eyes, afraid that they might fall upon something gruesome that I would never be able to forget. The fields that were crowded with Iraqi army personnel and vehicles when we arrived in Al-Suwayrah were now empty and desolate. Cautiously we kept away from the main highways and chose to take the agricultural routes instead, hoping to avoid American or Iraqi troops.

We had been told that we needed to post a white flag on the car to show our compliance and avoid attacks from the American marines. So I fastened one of Ameen's little blankets to the passenger window and prayed that it was visible. The roads were unpaved, dusty, and covered with ditches. Esam and his brother navigated possible routes, and we passed looters carrying away anything they had laid their hands on.

At one place I saw Uday Hussein's (Saddam's eldest son's) shiny purple and gold Mercedes being dragged upon the dirt road without tires. This was one of his iconic cars; we would see it parked at the Hunting Club or at the International School bazaars. The looters had tied it to another vehicle with ropes or chains and were struggling to pull it away; clouds of dust rose as the metal wheels scraped the dirt road.

As we neared Baghdad, the looting became more intense. People were looting everything, from plastic flowers and clothes to generators, refrigerators, air-conditioners, ovens, and furniture. We entered from Al-Dora, crossing the bridge near the oil refinery, and watched as the looters headed toward the luxurious houses along the Tigris. My husband, his eyes always alert, had repeatedly called out for me to put my head down or close my eyes, to keep me from witnessing something terrible, but I could not help myself. We were in a heightened state of alertness, afraid of becoming entangled in the violence and horror crossing with us along the bridge. It was in this state of bewilderment that I saw him.

Ahead of us, a pickup truck was awkwardly parked at an angle on our side of the road. The driver's door was ajar and the vehicle looked like it had been burning. It was charred on the roof and sides, its white paint now tainted black. On the road, next to the driver's open door, lay a man. He was dressed in a traditional Iraqi dishdasha, his head cover—shimagh and aqual—next to him on the ground. His body was bloated, the arms sprawled out, in surrender to some unseen enemy. The face was burned off, with no characteristics.

"Don't look!" Esam yelled, too late.

What amazed me was that no one on that road had stopped to cover the body, to stare at the man, to pity him, to mourn him. They walked right past him. He was just there, as though this was exactly where he should be on that road into Baghdad.

Smoke

a thick, black veil
rises from
the earth and the domes
of my burning
city

it crawls and conquers
ancient narrow alleyways, houses and shops
shrouding the city
in dust and rubble

it curls in streams
and hovers
over scorched
scattered bodies
longing for the kindness
of darting eyes
that choose to look
the other way

it tauntingly lingers
it whispers, it tugs

its tentacles tangled

in the strands of my hair

the soot plastered on my skin

black beads seep down my cheeks

fall against the ashes under

my feet

it rises from the fire inside me

The closer we got to our neighborhood, the greater our shock. So many of the buildings were still burning, their insides gutted and visible from the street, furniture and papers scattered around them. As we entered my brother-in-law's street, we saw Iraqi tanks impaled with poles and white flags, and discarded Iraqi army fatigues in piles on the street. The soldiers had surrendered or decided to flee in their undergarments, rather than face the Americans. I felt shame, but I also understood that our young soldiers were desperate and starving. Most of them were around eighteen years of age, still children, barely trained, and they had been put on the front lines.

Suddenly, we saw some American marines running toward us. My mouth dried up as I saw them raise their guns. In their uniforms and gear, they were like giants. One of them crept slowly toward the car. My baby was in my lap, fast asleep; I slowly raised him as the marine moved closer to my window. He momentarily looked at Ameen and shifted his eyes back at Esam. His intense blue eyes never left us for a second, nor did his gun. I know now that it was only seconds, but the moment seemed endless. I could not swallow or look away. My mind quickly played out the possibilities and found no comforting ending.

"My home! My home is here," Taha shouted through the open crack in the backseat window, breaking the silence. He pointed to his house at the end of the street and the marine finally waved his hand to let us go.

We left Taha to enter his house alone and headed toward our own home.

Home, April 2003

Exhausted from the journey—which normally took us less than an hour—we arrived having spent the whole day on the road. Our house had no windows on the first floor; they had all been shattered in the air raids, and there were only gaping holes left. Dust covered everything: the furniture, the marble floors, the antiques. We could not rest because we had to seal the house from animals and people before we could wash and rest.

Later, I sat on the edge of my bed, in our dark bedroom, feeding Ameen. I felt something crawl up my thigh. I jumped up screaming, quickly reaching for the flashlight, and saw a large American cockroach on my leg. I swiped it away and wondered what else might be lurking in the dark. I moved the flashlight around the room, pointing the light toward the corners and around the edges of the furniture to make sure nothing else was in that room with me.

I do not remember much of those first few days following the invasion. I know that we worked hard to clean the house, find clean food, and cope without running water and electricity. Prices of food staples had more than tripled; open, reliable stores were scarce. We had some canned meats, rice, and cooking oil still in the house, so we managed to make some meals. These were only to keep up our strength; we had lost our appetites and there was too much work to be done to ensure a safe and clean environment for the baby.

Amidst all these concerns, my mind was preoccupied with the well-being of my parents and my siblings. I had no knowledge of their whereabouts or even if they were alive. There were no working phones and the family was on the other side of the city: bridges, marines, and bodies lay between us. After debating where they could be, Esam finally decided that we drive across Baghdad to look for them.

The next day we drove into the frenzied streets; the routes that we usually used were either closed or destroyed. We tried a different route, through the old downtown and across Al-Joumhouria Bridge, but before we reached it a man came running toward us, urging us to stop. He had on a black vest imprinted with large white letters saying PRESS on its front.

"Don't cross the bridge!" he panted. "The Americans are shooting anyone who crosses. A whole family was just shot down in that car," he pointed toward the remains of a burning car on the bridge.

He looked at me and the baby, then turned to Esam. "Don't take them out with you. You shouldn't have them with you when you drive, it's too dangerous."

"We are looking for her family," my husband said. "She won't let me go alone."

"If you are heading to the other side of the city, you might be able to cross from Al-Sarafia Bridge. But I am not sure. Take her home. Go on your own." He looked my husband sternly in the eye.

As we began to drive away, we exchanged prayers with the man for safety and salvation. We found that Al-Sarafia Bridge was intact and there were no signs of American troops there. We sped across into Al-Utafia and Al-Iskan; we passed my college, which was desolate and covered in soot, like all the other buildings around it.

Soon after, we began to notice something awkward. Instead of the American presence, there were plainclothesmen behind sand barricades and what seemed to be some form of non-Iraqi resistance. Apparently this side of Baghdad had not fallen yet. Ahead of us stood a man in what seemed to be Pakistani or Afghan traditional dress; he had a long white beard and an RPG over his shoulder, and he was reading from what looked like a Quran in his other hand. We suddenly realized that he was waiting for the American tanks to cross the bridge.

"We are in the middle of a battlefield!" Esam shouted, his voice angry and fearful.

But I persisted that we continue; we were so close. And so he drove as fast as he could and we finally reached Al-Harthia. The area looked like it had been hit by chemical weapons. Nothing was moving; I could not even see birds or stray cats, which were usually everywhere. My parents' house looked abandoned. We banged on the high, cream-colored iron gate and waited. A while later, my father's driver came out and spoke to my husband quietly, as I strained to listen through the open car window. Esam returned and said that no one was home; they had not returned after the fall of Baghdad. My mind raced, wondering where they could be.

"Can we go to Amma Amel's house?" I asked quietly, knowing that I had crossed the border of sanity. He looked at me with confusion.

"We barely made it here alive. I don't know what is out there. Some parts on this side of the city haven't fallen and we could soon be in the midst of a battle."

"I know, but I am going to go crazy if I don't know where they are. Maybe Amma will know." I was desperate.

Reluctantly, he drove us toward my aunt's house in the Al-Qadisyia neighborhood, which was close to the main road that led to Saddam (now Baghdad) Airport. The roads were chocked with tanks, and the buildings were in ruins; the area looked like an actual battleground. The little shops on the main street were gaping black holes from the explosions and their sides were covered with bullet holes. No people were around. When we reached my aunt's house we saw a large hole in the concrete fence. There was no reply when we knocked. I inquired with the neighbors and was told that my aunt and her family left when the fighting became too intense. Esam insisted that we head back to our house.

Amma's house was on a main route taken by American troops. Later we learned that when they returned to their home, they found an Iraqi soldier's body in the yard and another in one of their parked cars. Men who had resisted the invading army were dragged through the streets tied to tanks. With all the passionate arguments against biological and chemical warfare that the Americans had broadcast in their propaganda before the invasion, one would think they would never use it in this invasion. According to my cousin Ali, Amma Amel's son, after the fall of Baghdad the airport and the highway leading to it were strewn with bodies of Iraqi soldiers covered in a yellow film. When they tried to lift them, the bodies fell apart in their hands. So the soldiers were buried where they had fallen along the highway.

———

For the next four days I busied myself with housework and the baby. One day, while clearing the living room, I saw a car stop in front of our gate. My brother's head surfaced over the gate, his eyes curiously scanning our house and yard. I screamed out his name. Afraid that he would disappear, I ran through the kitchen door and jumped on him, sobbing my incoherent thanks to God.

"We are all safe and back at the house in Al-Harthia," he said, hugging me.

"All of you, even Baba?" I asked through hot tears.

"Yes, we are all well. I swear," he replied. "You should all come. We should all be in one place."

My family had left for Baled, a small town to the north of Baghdad, with my brother's in-laws after they had holed up in their own house for as long as they could. The air raids had become too violent. They would hide in the pantry, off the kitchen, when the air raids began, all piled together in that small space. My mother compared the attacks to earthquakes. The ground beneath their feet would sway and move in waves. Their house was situated close to the Republican Palace compound. Everything around them was targeted.

Baghdad, April 2003

This time, as we drove through Baghdad toward my parents' home, I

was more focused on my surroundings and the depth of the destruction. The Americans had saved specific buildings, such as the Ministry
of Oil, and some of the buildings in the Republican Palace compound.
Everything else was fair game for the air raids and the looters. In Bab
al-Moatham, I saw the Library of Liberal Arts burning, and I recalled
with sadness all the times I had spent there studying. It was burned
three times. News began to spread about American troops breaking
down gates to government buildings with their tanks to let the looters
in. Even the National Museum of Iraq was not spared.

I am not sure which rumors were correct, but I do know that
the museum was pillaged. I can recall my only visit there with my
mother's brother, Khalo Ali, who was visiting from Russia a couple of
years before. The building had very few visitors because this was still
before its official reopening but we had been given clearance to enter.
We spent hours there; I even took my shoes off and walked barefoot
because my feet ached from all the walking. We saw artifacts that
dated all the way back to the Sumerians: small tools, jewelry, delicate
wooden sewing needles, detailed clay tablets with cuneiform script.
Most of the larger items, like the Code of Hammurabi, were taken
by Western excavators in the early twentieth century, so only repli-
cas were displayed. But walking through a history that spanned nearly
five thousand years of ancient and Islamic civilizations, including the
first form of writing, gave me a great sense of pride.

As we turned on Al-Tahrir Square roundabout in Al-Sadoun in
downtown Baghdad, we were faced with two bloodied teenagers
fighting with knives in the middle of the street; their clothes were
shredded and a woman behind them was heckling. I began to scream,
low and inaudible at first, and then with all my might. Esam asked me
repeatedly to calm down as he sped past them.

After we arrived at my parents' house, I spent the next few days in a
daze. I could not believe my family was safe and alive. I was so grateful, but also so broken by all the loss and destruction and the sudden

and interminable changes that had taken place in our lives.

Everyone had to stay inside the house; we could not go back to our routines as we had done after the first Gulf War. Esam and I stayed with my family for a few days. He could not return to work and neither could any of my family members. My father had heard that the research facility and the poultry farms that he had directed had been burned down by looters. Haydar and Sara, who were both in the middle of completing their medical residencies to become physicians, were unable to go back to the hospitals where they worked. Shayma had been a couple of months shy of her BSc in biology, but was told now that she might have to repeat the year. Our lives came to a halt; the days melded into each other with our listlessness and confusion.

———

Videos began to emerge of the former government's tortures and executions. The media showed everything they could get their hands on, without censorship or warning; image after image of mass executions and killings. Even older photographs, of executions and assassinations that had been taken during the Ba'ath revolution, were discussed and analyzed. The one I remember the most was the photo and story of the execution of Abd al-Karim Qasim, who became prime minister after the July 14 revolution that overthrew the monarchy in 1958. While growing up, I had heard many stories about Qasim. My mother idolized him for being a patriotic man who championed the working classes and supported education for all. In my parents' living room, I watched with my father as one of the news networks broadcast the interviews with witnesses detailing the plot to remove Qasim in 1963.

"What moved me the most about his death," recalled one of the interviewees, "was his demeanor and bravery when they came to execute him. He asked for a moment to straighten his military uniform and his side cap. Then he sat down on a chair, as if waiting for them to take his photograph."

I turned to my father, who sighed heavily in the chair next to me. I was sure he had heard this story, but he was shaking his head as if he was hearing it for the first time.

"All we have known is violence. When will we ever know peace? Will we ever have a generation that knows peace and security?" I asked, my voice high-pitched and shaking.

"It's a dark history," my father replied without moving his eyes from the television screen.

"But why? Why do we have to live like this? Will it ever end?" I left the room crying hysterically. I ran toward the kitchen, and I could hear him following me.

"You have to stop now," he said. "You cannot act like this. Be stronger. You will see much more of this. What you saw was from a half century ago; you can't be in hysterics every time something comes up."

He stood in the kitchen doorway, looking at me sternly.

I sobbed, "I can't do this anymore. I can't. It's unfair."

"Everyone is going through this. You are not the only one. You have to be stronger." He turned around and left me to gather myself.

I sat down at the kitchen table feeling berated for reacting, trying to understand why he was so upset with me. I think he wanted us to stay strong because he did not want us to give in to the madness around us. He wanted us to be strong, so he could stay strong.

———

Al-Jazeera and Al-Arabiya news channels competed for the most shocking and most violent stories they could find. People began to talk about Americans freeing prisoners from the basements of the Intelligence Agency, and rumors of naked men, beaten and delusional, running through the streets, began to surface.

Then they discovered the mass graves, some from the 1991 uprisings. They began uncovering mounds of remains that included women and children. People began to visit the sites in hopes of finding any material evidence that would lead them to the remains of their loved ones. Women in black abayas lined up in the copper-colored dust with documents and pictures of their sons, brothers, and fathers who had disappeared, and waited for the remains to be carefully laid out and tagged—piles of bones to distinguish from other piles of bones. I watched them on television and wondered how they could recognize them.

For thirty years and through three major wars and thirteen years of sanctions, we had remained silent out of fear for ourselves and our loved ones. We had been numbed by the brutality and senselessness of Saddam Hussein's government and its unlimited thirst for power.

That silence now condemned us.

From My Diary

April 28 2003

I think I only have a few minutes before the baby wakes up again. My life has become hectic and monotonous. The same occurrences over and over again without rest or peace of mind. I don't even have time to think.

It's Saddam Hussein's birthday today but there's nobody to celebrate it, he's been overthrown. I'm writing by lamp light [sic], there's no power and the US never seem [sic] to stop. The fighting is over but the aftermath seems worse. I can't really see what I'm writing, maybe I'll finish it off tomorrow? If the baby gives me time. He's so beautiful but so much work.

Baghdad, May 2003

One day while I was at my parents' house, my father came home exhausted, his lips blue with anger and disgust. He had recently gone back to work to try and salvage his department and the research he had worked on for the last thirteen years. His department, which was concerned with poultry nutrition, was in one of the buildings that was looted and burned; even live hens were burned in the process. During his drive back home, an American tank rammed into his car; the tank moved forward and dragged him along with it. The soldiers did not notice, until people in the street began shouting. When they stopped and unhitched the car, they carelessly told him that it was his fault and he did not know how to drive. He then pulled out his American-issued license, which he had begun to carry with him in case he was pulled over; he told them, sarcastically, that he was seen fit enough to drive by their own government. The soldiers shrugged away his angry protest and moved on.

My father felt violated in his own streets by "boys" less than half his age. That was his breaking point. He decided that he could no longer stay in Iraq and began making arrangements to leave for Amman, Jordan and have my mother and sister follow him later.

From My Diary

June 18 2003

The easiest way out of all this is a bullet straight in the head. Everyone is so tired of the situation, the power was shut off for 18 hours today & there may be another cut in 2 hours. I don't know how we are still sane?!

It's like living in a huge cell, no way out and the sentence is forever. It's like 30 years under Saddam's rule wasn't enough torture for these people[;] they have to go through all this.

My dad is sending for my mom in 10 days. I don't know if her leaving is right. She's had a bad time, but can she leave us alone? Especially [my sister]. She needs rest, a little fresh air and a change of mood. But I don't think she can stay abroad with us here.

Baghdad, June 2003

I begged Esam to take us out in the car for a drive and maybe pick up some food from one of the restaurants that had reopened. I felt imprisoned inside the house, with no electricity, no continuous running water, and a tiny, colicky baby who rarely stopped crying. I was exhausted and bored out of my mind. The home that I had cherished had become a curse.

We needed to leave before the curfew began at sundown. The Americans had enforced curfews in Baghdad to control people's movements and prevent attacks on their patrolling convoys. Civilians tried to reach their destinations before that time anyway because of the threats that came with nightfall: gangs, marines, criminals. I sat next to him in the car, quietly content after leaving the stifling boredom of the house. My son lay sleeping in my lap. When we arrived at the restaurant, we saw American soldiers buying sandwiches.

Esam looked at me intensely. "I told you we should not leave the house. Stay in the car. I'll get take-out." He waited until the Americans had left to order our meal.

We had tried our best to avoid the soldiers. Less contact, less trouble. Recently, they were being attacked during their expeditions through the city and anyone around them was in danger.

Esam brought the sandwiches, and we ate them in the car on our way back home. He must have seen the look of despair and anxiety on my face as we neared our house in the dark street.

He said, "Maybe we should take a drive around the street until they turn the neighborhood generator on. I don't want to go back into the dark house."

Some people had begun to invest in large generators—250 KVA or more—and sell units of amperes to the houses in the neighborhood. Most nights we could not see our hands in front of our faces because of the extreme darkness. Esam would wake up at night struggling to breathe, yelling that he felt like he was trapped in a coffin.

The street was empty and dusk had just settled in. Ahead of us was a large ditch in the road; Esam swore under his breath and slowed down to avoid it. Just as we slowed down, a white sedan cut us off. All its doors opened, and five men with machine guns appeared.

The incident took place in a few seconds. We had had repeated conversations before on handling such scenarios. Esam would emphasize, "Immediately get out and give them the car. Don't act brave. All they want is the car." But his reaction that day was different; I think he feared what they would do to us.

I remember holding my son close to my chest   and turning
   my body
around   my back a buffer against any bullets   that could
   strike through the windshield.
I crouched down,
squeezing myself between the front seat and the dashboard,
saying verses from the Quran,
asking Allah to protect us, "Ya rab, ya rab!"
My baby whimpered,
but went silent, as if he knew we couldn't make a sound.
Esam put the transmission into reverse.
My body rammed into the passenger seat
as the car flew backward.
Esam placed his hand on my head,
pushing me further onto the floor of the car.
I can't remember if he told me to stay down.
I think I was screaming.
Or was that in my head?
We hit something that made the car lurch.
Maybe a brick? I hope it's a brick.

We entered our street.
I am definitely screaming.
I see armed men jump over our neighbors' fence—our neighbors' bodyguards.
Did they really jump over a five-foot fence?
I'm not sure about that memory anymore.

My subconscious must have interpreted the bodyguards as
heroes.
So the scene plays out like a movie in my mind.
Our car doors open,
our neighbors hold us tight,
neighbors we hardly knew.
They took away my screaming baby,
echoing my own screams.

I remember water being splashed on my face.
I remember a neighbor reading verses from the Quran in my
ear,
to calm me down. Verses I was never able to complete.
I remember cursing those men.
Cursing their mothers.
Cursing our lives.

I couldn't stop screaming.
I still hear that scream.
I still see those moments,
as if watching from outside my body.
I am not sure how we got away.

That night Esam decided that we had to find a way out, out of this
madness and instability, out of a country that was no longer our own.

We sat in our living room huddled together, the baby between us.
We cried out of gratitude and fear all at once, knowing that inevitably
we would one day leave this home. We realized that this part of our
life was coming to an end. Everything that we had tried to cling to
since the invasion began was pushing us away. So many people had
fled, so many of those who had remained were changed from loss and
deprivation. We were strangers in our own country.

As the days passed, that sense of dislocation grew.

My father left for Jordan in May 2003. Our first trip to Amman was in July that same year, when we took my mother to join him. There were no flights between Baghdad and Amman, so we traveled in a GMC SUV. The drive usually took ten hours through the desert, but our talkative Palestinian Jordanian driver had told us to expect delays due to bandits and American military caravans that forbade drivers to pass them or follow too closely behind. So I added a couple more items to my list of things that I would need. I prepared our bags, washed, and prayed.

I sat on the sijada (prayer rug) and begged God earnestly for a safe journey. As we left before dawn, I looked back at the house and cried. Esam had told me that if we found a way to stay in Amman, we would not return.

The road was dark as we began to leave the city, passing Abu Ghraib, a smaller city on the edge of Baghdad. The Abu Ghraib torture scandal had not yet happened, but the whole area from there to Al-Falluja was tense with resistance groups and American attacks. This was also the road to the Habbaniyah and Therthar lakes, where our families had spent vacations on the beaches and the resorts. Both areas had been attacked and heavily looted.

We had not left Baghdad since the invasion; the farthest we had been was Suwayrah. The driver sped through the towns and as daylight broke, we found that the road snaked through a vast empty desert. There were few other cars, but we noticed that a couple had kept very close to ours. The driver increased his speed and said, "Those are bandits."

We looked at the car speeding by us and saw two heavily built men with thick, black mustaches. Driving as fast as he could, our driver kept swerving on the road, shifting from side to side, a maneuver used to avoid being stopped by other cars. We held on tightly to the armrests and I pulled my baby closer. Eventually, the other cars lost interest, and our driver let out a loud sigh of relief. "Alhamdulillah! I thought they would never quit."

He sped ahead and cheerfully chatted with my husband about Jordan, his family in Palestine, and regional politics, until we arrived at the Trabil border crossing. The line of cars was long and slow; but the driver quickly took our passports and went to see the border officials. I would cross this border many times later, and while I do not remember all the drivers or the journeys, this one has stood out for me. We had heard that people were often sent back from the border, and we were filled with anxiety, but this turned out to be our fastest crossing into Jordan.

The driver returned with our documents and gave us his phone to use to contact my father, who was stunned at the speed at which we had crossed.

We arrived at Le Royal Hotel in Amman, where my father was staying, just before dusk. It was a monumental hotel, a tall round tower amidst a spread of tiny houses and shops. I felt like I had stepped into the future. The doormen and bellhops ran to pick up our very outdated pieces of luggage—we looked like we had stepped out of the 1980s. It seemed like a decade had passed since my last visit to Amman the year before. I had recently broken my toe, which was wrapped in bandages, so I hobbled along into the hotel lobby feeling tired, dusty, and old. We entered the elevator to find a young woman with a sparkling pink evening gown and long black hair. I hid behind my tall husband, wishing that I was invisible.

In Amman, my father tried to establish a business and Esam tried to find a job. When Haydar, Sara, and Shayma arrived a short time later, we all packed ourselves into a small, cheaply furnished apartment. My father would not accept any help with the rent, so we tried to find ways to contribute, like buying groceries and running errands. This would be the last time that we would all live under one roof.

A couple of months later, Haydar and Sara left Amman to live in

England. Since Sara was half British, they believed that they would be able to establish themselves there and go back to completing their training as physicians. She was also pregnant and they needed to travel as soon as possible to ensure that they settled before the baby arrived.

Esam and I began to think about leaving Jordan as well, but we had no concrete plans to follow. We met with an immigration lawyer in Amman, who told us the process would take about four years and would initially cost around five thousand US dollars. As we left her office, we discussed our options. We felt that we could not afford to give away that kind of money for an uncertain outcome. What if our application failed? We had no source of income and we were living on our savings; we had no idea how long it would take to find jobs.

We made the decision to apply for a visa to England and stay with my brother to figure things out. We had heard that Iraqis were applying for refugee status in some of the European countries. But we could not find a way to remain in England legally; and we became hesitant and afraid of the unknown. Our trip was a momentary escape from the situation back home and those weeks away allowed us to see that there was hope for a more settled life abroad.

We returned to Amman after one month and headed for Baghdad almost immediately. Esam needed to find a stable source of income; staying in Jordan was costing us money we could not afford. As we headed back to Baghdad on that terrible road, my heart was heavy with separation and dread. Back in Baghdad we tried to settle down and resume the life we had before the war. Esam finally got a job close to our home. With difficulty, we found a way to live through the uncertain conditions and tried to get back to some form of normal life.

Americans in Baghdad 2003

American presence had become more prevalent; their military

caravans roamed our streets, they stopped at local restaurants and bakeries for meals, they tried to manage traffic and checkpoints. They would sometimes wave to the children and smile at us as we passed by in our cars. One time, I lifted my hand to wave back and stopped abruptly, reprimanding myself for being foolish. We tried to avoid any interaction with American soldiers, fearing their reactions and the reactions of Iraqis who refused to accept their presence.

Once, when my mother was still in Iraq, an American soldier stopped her and Shayma at a checkpoint and asked them, "Aren't you happy that we are here to liberate you from a dictator?"

When my mother replied, "No," the soldier was stunned. My mother and sister then explained to him all that we had lost. His concept of liberation was naive. The number of war casualties was immense; entire families had been killed in their homes during the air raids. Some areas in the capital had been reduced to rubble and the country's infrastructure was destroyed. Our outlook for a better, "democratic" government was bleak and somewhat futile under those conditions. We had been liberated from one government, only to be under the mercy of a military presence that had no regard for the people's interests.

One day while I was at a toy store, I met a female soldier who approached me to play with Ameen. She was fully armed, very tall, and intimidating. I stood quietly as she told me that she had left her own two-month baby girl behind. When she finished playing with my baby's tiny fingers, I asked her, "Why did you leave her?"

She replied, angry and confused, "Because I was needed here. That's a stupid question."

Her face was stern. Her duty was to be here, thousands of miles away from her daughter in order to "save" the Iraqi people. I had just questioned the whole basis of her service and duty. I was an ungrateful Iraqi, who did not understand the sacrifices she had made. She moved toward the door with a look of disgust on her face.

Somewhere deep inside me, I pitied them. I saw the soldiers as young, raw, and inexperienced, serving in smoldering heat that left their faces burning red. Always fully clothed in their fatigues and gear. It must have been unbearable. I kept thinking about their mothers back home, anxious for their return. As a new mother, I was conflicted in my feelings toward them, but I feared them just the same.

All the uncertainty and instability in Iraq led to the rise of organized insurgency, which began to attack both the American troops and the Iraqis who worked for them. This kept the Americans on edge. They were always on guard and ceased to roam the streets freely. People began spreading news about soldiers who became frantic and began shooting at crowds in the streets. Once I overheard Esam telling a friend about an American soldier who had dragged an Iraqi man out of his car because the man would not reply to his questions. The man was beaten in public, and no one was able to help him. As Esam related the experience, I could sense the bitterness in his voice and the utter desperation.

Even though some like to believe that the first Gulf War in 1991, the thirteen years of imposed sanctions, and the American invasion in 2003 were not related, for many of us they were all related, connected and planned. In 1991 the Iraqi people still felt loyalty for their country, and by the end of the Iran-Iraq war, for many, Saddam still was a powerful and effective ruler. The sanctions ended that loyalty and support for him. Hunger, privation, and loss pushed the Iraqis to the edge, where they thought that anything other than Saddam would be better.

From 1991 the Americans had two main goals: weaken the Iraqi presence in the region and control its oil reserves. They have achieved both. Sometimes I hear Iraqis who despised Saddam say that they would take him back any day, instead of all the destruction, violence and loss that the Americans unleashed on our country.

The Aftermath

There was utter lawlessness and banditry. Anti-Saddam elements went on killing sprees, wiping out former government officials, members of the Ba'ath Party, and the ex-military. Ba'ath Party members and supporters of Saddam turned to active resistance. Killings took place in the streets, in homes, and through bombings of public spaces. There was a rise in kidnappings and killings of intellectuals and professionals. The stories that circulated about these murders and abductions were atrocious.

A close friend of my father and a well-known surgeon was kidnapped for ransom. He had left the hospital in Baghdad, along with his bodyguards, but soon they found themselves closely followed and then surrounded by several cars. As the driver tried to accelerate, one of the kidnappers pulled out an RPG. At that point the surgeon surrendered but asked for his driver and bodyguards to be released. His wife paid the off the kidnappers and mercifully he was returned to his family. Esam and I visited him at his home. His face was bruised beyond recognition; his eyes were bloody masses, the skin around them dark blue and swollen. But at least he had been released, and he was thankful for that.

We heard about other friends and acquaintances who were kidnapped or killed. One of them was the University of Baghdad's Dean of Medicine.

> He had sat in our home.
> Dined with my family.
> A tall man with gentle eyes and a big personality.
> I had watched him give the convocation speech at my brother's
>   graduation.
> The graduating class chanted his name; they adored him.
> A man walked into his office,
> in his clinic,
> shot him once in the head.

Later, a family friend's son was kidnapped
from his home.
He was 25.
They asked for a ransom.
The negotiations went on for a while.
Then they left a gunny bag
by his parents' gate.
He was inside,
in pieces.

About a year after the young man's death, I sat across from his
mother, a friend of the family, at the dining table in my parents' backyard in Amman. At the time, I did not know about the incident. The
mother was draped in black, the color of mourning. During those days
most women were dressed in black. The woman began to describe her
son's kidnapping and murder, all the disturbing details about how they
found his remains, all the time sounding as casual as though discussing recipes and home décor.

"They brought me the DVD," she finally said. "They caught the
men who kidnapped him and I saw them on the DVD," she explained,
a grim smile crossing her face.

I realized that she was talking about how her son's murder had been
avenged. "They" were the kidnappers. Were the kidnappers executed
on the DVD? Had she paid someone to find and kill them? I was
unsettled by the thought that this gentle woman would plot such a
thing. I did not ask. I did not utter a word. I let her speak, sensing the
urge she had to disclose these details, to let them flow out of her. As
though this act of telling, not of vengeance, would in some way restore
her son to her.

———

The number of dead bodies reached 1,500 a day at one point. There were frequent news reports of bodies found floating in the river in gunny bags. The stories piled up. They were unfathomable and absurdly violent; it was not just the killings but mindless butchery, as though life had no meaning left at all. Finally, I stopped listening and my family stopped recounting them to me.

On American news networks, broadcasters would relate the names of their men killed in combat and they would show pictures of them looking smart in their uniforms, often with their families and their dogs; they would tell stories about their bravery and the sacrifices they had made for their nation. But in Iraq, the dead were piled up on the roadside, in pickup trucks, in hospital morgues. So many, that families had to dig through the piles when searching for their missing. It had become a routine.

A killing would take place or an IED go off and people picked up the bodies or their parts from the roads and the sidewalks, they hosed off the blood and remains, buried them and then reopened their stores and went about their business as usual.

Nightmares

She came to the Moses basket beside my bed and carried away Ameen without telling me. All I could see was the curly, blonde hair and the white arms that carried the bundle. From her accent, I knew she was American. Somehow my subconscious created a social worker, someone from my childhood memories, or the endless American films on the satellite channels.

"Wait! He's mine!" I cried.

"No, it's not safe, I have to take him away. This is not a healthy environment." She smiled cunningly.

I woke up crying, afraid to look at the basket. I kept reassuring myself how utterly impossible it was for this to actually happen. I was shivering uncontrollably. I knew there was a flashlight on the bedside table, yet I was afraid to move or turn toward the little basket next to me. The darkness of the room was heavy and binding.

I knew he was not there.

I shook Esam awake. He turned on the flashlight that he kept next to him.

"Please, look into the basket!"

"Why?"

"She took him! Please!" I urged, digging my nails into his flesh.

He leaned across me toward the basket, put out his hand to feel the baby. "He's fine, he's sleeping."

Elections 2005

The first time I was able to vote, we were still under Saddam's rule. My father took us to the polling station in Al-Karrada. The ballot had one candidate: Saddam Hussein. Voters were required to check "Yes" or "No" in response to the question, which asked if he should be president.

My father had warned us in the car, "Check the box next to the "Yes" on the ballot. Do not try to joke around or be daring. It will be considered an act of treason if you choose to check the other box. Do not speak with anyone, just check the box." I could tell that he was anxious. The atmosphere in Baghdad was tense, maybe because the public was apparently given the opportunity to practice a democratic right, but they knew very well that the outcome would be the same no matter what box was checked on the ballot.

At the station, there was a single cardboard box on a table in the middle of the room to collect the ballots. Ba'athist organizers stood close to the table and watched what we checked on the ballot before we could place it in the box. The entire process was ridiculous.

When Izzat al-Douri—the Vice Chairman of the Iraqi Revolutionary Command Council—came out on television to declare the unanimous win for Hussein, we laughed.

At a dinner at my parents' house, I overheard a woman say, "The organizers took out the ballots and made sure that they all had check marks next to the 'Yes' option. They changed the ones that did not."

When Esam and I discussed this issue, he said that his family had voted twice because they received ballots for two different stations. "We feared that if we did not go to either one of them we would be taken by the Mukhabarat," he explained.

On December 15 2005, when our parliamentary elections took place, the atmosphere was quite different. People were excited to participate in the process, even though few had hopes for real change or development.

Esam, Ameen, and I walked to the polling station at a nearby school in Zayouna. Fearing bombings and violent outbreaks, the interim government had banned the use of any kind of vehicles for the day.

As we left the school, Caroline Hawley, a BBC correspondent, approached me.

"Do you speak English?" she asked.

"Yes, I do," I replied with a smile. I had seen her on the news networks and felt like I was speaking to a celebrity.

"Would you be open to answering some questions about the elections?"

"Uh, sure." I looked at Esam, who nodded.

She listed some of her questions and then asked, "Are you Sunni or Shia?"

"I am Shia, but I will not answer that question on air," I pursed my lips.

"Why?"

"I do not think that it's important. We are all eager to be part of this election."

I hated the way Westerners kept emphasizing the sectarian differences between us. I have a recording of that quick interview; in it I can see the glimpse of hope I had as I spoke about our need for a stable government and basic living needs. I believed that the next government would work toward rebuilding the country and repairing the infrastructure. Unfortunately, that has not been the case so far.

Baghdad 2004 or 2005

I can't remember the date.
It was night, it was summer.
I open the gray, iron gate
and I am face to face
with an African American man in army fatigues.
The helmet partly sliding down to his eyes.
My eyes look down
into the barrel of the gun
he holds close to my face.
I notice the slight shiver in his hand.
I notice that that shiver is contagious.
I lift my eyes.
Our eyes lock.
My mind races saying prayers and pleas.
Does he see my eyes pleading?
He breaks that moment of stillness
and silence,
looking back toward others in the shadows behind him.
And I move slightly.
The texture of the paint,
the gray paint on the iron door,
is somewhat flaky and warm
and damp under my palm.
I silently and with great caution,
as if in slow motion,

try to close the door,
carefully, without force, without the click,
without aggression, without fear,
and more importantly, without hate.
My knees fold,
and I am on the tiles of our driveway.
I sit and wait and think it will pass.
Finally light footsteps pass the gate.
They move in the darkness of the unlit streets that fill my fallen
city.

SIX

Baghdad 2005

Esam came home one day with a page from *Al-Sabah*.

"Look, there is a program through the American government for studying abroad," he said, pointing to the call for applications. I briefly glanced at the page and went back to stirring the pot on the stove. I did not believe that an opportunity like that was really attainable.

"Just take a look at it," he shoved the page in front of me again.

The posting was for a Fulbright Scholarship to complete a master's degree in the United States. I think I laughed out as I read through. The situation in Iraq had left me hopeless for any kind of future. The year that we married I had just received my MA in English Literature from the University of Baghdad. It was three years since those nights of studying and analyzing John Fowles's novels for my thesis. The invasion and the aftermath had left me a full-fledged housewife and mother. My interests lay solely in rearranging furniture and teaching my toddler to speak English.

"You think they would choose people like us? With all the corruption around us, we are the last people they would give this to," I said, putting down the paper.

The new Iraqi government was neck-deep in corruption. Each cabinet member had his own militia to take out his opposition; they worked like gangs, threatening people, turning them out of their homes, building concrete fortresses throughout the city. They did nothing for the Iraqi people except cause division. We had feared one dictator, now we had dozens.

"I think you should apply. This could be our way out of this hell. How is Ameen going to grow up here?" He looked at me with concern. He was right. Since the invasion, we had tried to find ways to leave Baghdad. We had tried to find work in Amman but without success. We were afraid of anything that was illegal and the processes for gaining residency anywhere abroad seemed daunting.

Our neighborhood was slowly turning into a ghost town, as families packed and left the country or moved to cities in Kurdistan in search of safety and stability. At one point, it seemed that we were the only family on our street. Even the sole close friend I had made during the past couple of years—Luna—had decided that it was too dangerous to stay. Her husband's job as head of a company had not helped them, and the company had even been raided. They lived in constant fear for their children. As Christians, they felt more threatened, both by insurgents and by fanatical religious groups. Her brother had been kidnapped and beaten, and later her eighteen-year-old cousin had been kidnapped, strangled, and disposed of on a roadside. He had been a student at the School of Medicine. They had asked around, searched in the streets, and visited hospital morgues. Finally, his mother went to look though the bodies at the morgue and identified his body through a birthmark on his neck.

No Tags, No Walls

they have no tags
around their tanned necks

the beaded metal
is not
embedded in their flesh
no names
engraved
telling us to whom
they once belonged

there are no walls
on which their
names shine

there are only dismembered bodies
with eyes bound
to clear blind skies

we search for signs
a small birthmark on his neck
a white shirt
a black shoe

the only features listed:
hands bound,
blindfolded
execution style
floating in the Tigris
floating

Luna's departure left me desolate. Since the invasion, families had avoided leaving their homes and neighborhoods for fear of being attacked. The situation had become so dire that every time we left the house, we would pack an overnight bag and strategize which family we could stay with if the curfew began before we could reach home. I cannot count the number of times we found ourselves stuck in traffic, face to face with the blasting rifles of militias or convoys of American Hummers and tanks. Once, my husband called his brother in the middle of one of these militia outbursts to tell him of the street on which he would find our bodies.

The only way I got through that first year was because of Luna and her family. The blackouts were much easier to endure together and we found ways to entertain ourselves with barbecues and movie nights while the generators were running. We even overcame our fears of the violence around us by just being together. One night we were in their yard having dinner while the kids ran around playing. Suddenly we heard a whistle, then an RPG missile hit the side of a house two doors down. Debris flew into the yard, into our plates and our hair. We picked up the kids and ran quickly into the kitchen. After a few silent minutes of suspense, we came back outside; we dusted off our clothes, took out clean plates, and went on as before. If we were going to die, we would do it while enjoying a good barbecue.

After Luna moved with her children to Amman, I was once again alone. Ameen would repeatedly ask if we could cross the street to their house. He had become very attached to her children. On days when we could not leave the house due to excessive violence in the streets, he would sit with his face glued to the living room window and look longingly outside. I struggled to keep him busy and entertained. I began teaching him English and simple math. We filled his room with all kinds of toys to keep him engaged. But some days he was so bored with staying indoors and being alone that he would cry himself to sleep.

On good days, he would go outside the house with our driver, a man in his late sixties, and play with the stray cats that came into the yard. I have pictures of him in a blue and white t-shirt, diapers, and tiny black leather sandals playing with Abu Abbas and a stray orange cat. He always thought it was his cat.

One day he was sitting next to our large window in the living room, talking to the cat through the glass pane. An explosion went off nearby just as I was leaving the room; it was deafening. I turned and ran toward him, anticipating the window to shatter, just as a shock wave traveled through my body and into the rest of the house. I pulled him away from the window; his face had lost all color and his eyes were struggling to read my own. Then he let out a cry.

Our Way Out

Esam kept reminding me of the scholarship and finally convinced me to apply. Over the next few months we began to put together my application and collect the documents we needed for submission. Finally I received an email informing me that I had been shortlisted for an interview with the Fulbright selections committee in the Green Zone.

August 2005

> Dear Fulbright Applicant
>
> We are pleased to inform you that you have been chosen to be interviewed for the 2006-07 Fulbright Competition!
>
> Following the interviews, the Fulbright-Iraq Bi-National Selection Committee will nominate the top Iraqi candidates to the U.S. Department of State.
>
> Your interview will take place on **August 27** at the U.S. Embassy.
>
> To take part in the interviews, you must be at the Information Desk in the Baghdad Convention Center by 8:30 AM. **THERE ARE NO EXCEPTIONS TO THIS REQUIREMENT.** If you are not at the Information Desk in the Convention Center at this time, you will not be interviewed, so, PLEASE ALLOW AM-

PLE TIME FOR YOUR TRAVEL TO THE CON-
VENTION CENTER.

In the event that the Convention Center is closed or
you are denied passage through the checkpoint for any
reason, please contact us at Iraqna: 0790 18

Please bring two Iraqi identification (ID) cards with
you (your passport and national ID card). Be prepared
for long lines to get through the checkpoint (allow
at least 30 minutes to get to the check point). At the
checkpoint, everyone is searched by the guards before
they are allowed to walk to the Convention Center, so
be prepared for this as well.

The best preparation for the interview is for you to go
over your Personal Statement and Study Objective in
your application and be prepared to talk about: (1) your
proposed field of study in the United States, and (2)
how this will help your country when you return. Another good question is how do you think an American
campus will benefit from your presence there for two
years.

Good luck on the interview—you are part of a most
select group of Iraqi scholars and we welcome the opportunity to speak with you!

The Green Zone, previously the area that contained the official complex of the Republican Palace and the homes of the President's family
and high government officials, had become a center for American oper-
ations in Baghdad. The site was heavily guarded and extremely intimidating. The hierarchy of power was very clear in the way the fortress
was secured—the "least" important soldiers were at the outer gates.
A gradually ascending hierarchy of importance and power proceeded
with each inner gate, beginning with Iraqis securing the outer gates and
Americans at the core. This area, like others around the city, was protected by concrete walls several feet high built around it.

Going through the streets in Baghdad was like negotiating a maze; we were unable to see anything behind the walls on the way and were prohibited from entering certain areas that were once civilian neighborhoods. Just seeing these walls brought me anxiety. Esam dropped me off at the gates of the Green Zone, which meant that anyone could see me entering. People had been killed for any kind of interaction with the Americans, even for simple things like selling them produce or bread. Everyone looked like a threat to me as Esam and Ameen left me at that outer gate.

I went through the checkpoints hesitantly, trying my best to avoid eye contact. In such a conservative culture, we feared soldiers assaulting women or touching them inappropriately during searches at checkpoints. People were outraged that women were patted down by male soldiers; the sight of older women in traditional abayas being manhandled in that way raised even more anger toward the Americans. The humiliation and disgrace of being touched by some strange man kept women from leaving their homes except for necessities. So I prayed under my breath that they would only need to check my bag.

Inside, the complex was well organized, relatively clean, and safe. We were asked to gather at a certain area and the coordinator called for our attention. She was a short, cheerful, and energetic Iraqi woman and she tried to explain the details of the schedule for the upcoming interviews. Our nervous commotion and constant interruptions forced her to stand up on a bench to hold our attention.

"I am not allowed to be up here because they fear that we become easy targets," she laughed nervously. After a few minutes, we calmed down, but remained wary of unseen threats. We were excited to be selected, but conscious of the danger of being seen in this place.

A small bus took us to our next destination. A heavily built American driver, who in his leather vest and white goatee looked more like a biker, smiled at us as we boarded. I had never been in this area before, since during Saddam's time access had been limited to government officials and their family members and close friends; the general public was allowed inside only during celebrations. As we drove through the inner streets I observed that most of the buildings and white-stone mansions had been attacked, most likely during the air raids. Some streets looked completely desolate; in the past three years no rebuilding had taken place.

The bus stopped in front of what had been the home of the Prince Regent during the time of King Faisal II, who had ruled Iraq before the 1958 revolution against the British-sponsored monarchy. Unlike the other buildings and mansions in the complex, this house was simple and smaller in size; it had been renovated and had central air-conditioning.

I was nervous entering the interview room, not knowing what to expect. The panel was made up of Iraqis and Americans, who calmly asked me questions about my academic background and the reasons behind my interest in pursuing a degree. They noticed my North American accent and showed interest in my application. As the conversation moved to my hobbies and experiences, I began to chat comfortably about my keenness to help develop the education system in Iraq. I forgot about my desire to flee the country and actually believed that my voice mattered and that I could make a difference. I spoke about how we had been burdened by the years of isolation from the world due to the sanctions and the wars. In that air-conditioned room, filled with smiling, inquisitive faces, in the middle of the Green Zone, I planted a seed of hope in my desperate mind for a settled and developed Iraq.

———

The application process took close to a year. I completed the requirements and passed every subsequent exam and interview, while still caring for my young child. The main challenge was getting to the venues. Due to the curfews and continuing violence, there were exam cancellations, delays, and changes in locations. The GRE was postponed a couple of times. The Babylon Hotel, now the Babylon Warwick Hotel, in Karrada was chosen for its venue; the room had floor to ceiling windows, which we candidates could not help looking at constantly, fearing that an explosion nearby would kill us all just from the shattered glass. While the exam was difficult, my fear of being maimed by broken glass was far greater.

October 19 2005

Dear Fulbright Scholar:

It gives us great pleasure to inform you of your selection as a principal grantee for a Fulbright Student Scholarship to study in the United States.

Through this scholarship award, you will pursue academic study toward a graduate degree and join Fulbright students from across the globe in a unique educational and cultural experience.

The 2006 Fulbright-Iraq competition marks the third time this scholarship has been offered in Iraq since the program was reinstated in November 2003. The selection committees reviewed many highly qualified candidates from all over Iraq. Your selection is a reflection of your outstanding personal and academic qualifications.

Please be aware that certain conditions must be met in order to finalize your scholarship. The Institute of International Education (IIE) in New York, the agency responsible for your academic placement and general administration of your grant, will explain these conditions to you and guide you through the entire placement process. You will be hearing from them very shortly.

Thank you for your interest in the Fulbright Program and for your persistence in applying for the 2006 scholarship under challenging circumstances. Please accept our best wishes for continued success in completing the final steps to becoming a Fulbright Scholarship student from Iraq.

You will be receiving more information from us soon with detailed instruction regarding your application and the visa process.

Please confirm receipt of this notification letter when you receive it.

Sincerely,
Fulbright Iraq

At this same time, Esam began looking for a way to join me if I was accepted. He applied to Kansas State University as an international student and was accepted in the graduate program of the Department of Grain Science and Industry. We were in Amman when he received his acceptance letter and we lost our minds with disbelief and happiness. We were blessed to leave the country together, instead of being separated.

We had been rescued from the madness.

Baghdad, February 2006

Iraq had been officially secular until the American invasion, when we began to witness the first signs of sectarian violence. Immediately after the fall of Baghdad, we heard about scattered sectarian killings taking place. But it was not until February 2006, when bombs were detonated at the Al-Imam, Al-Hadi, and Al-Askari shrines in Samarra, that a very noticeable shift in tolerance took place. The destruction of the shrines, sacred to Shia Muslims, ignited a civil war between the Shia and Sunni Muslims in the country. In the months following the invasion, Sunni and Shia imams and their followers would walk arm in arm in peace rallies to show the public that they were one, united people. Nevertheless, people began to be slaughtered according to their names and the neighborhoods in which they lived, without any consideration for the long history of tolerance and unity.

March 2006

Following my acceptance, I received an email invitation:

> Dear Fulbrighters:
>
> We hope that all is well with each of you.
>
> Please make plans now to attend a special luncheon on March 13 in Baghdad.
>
> Ambassador Zalmay Khalilzad has been invited to speak to you as a group.

"We would like you to sit at the Ambassador's table," a white American woman in her late twenties said to me when I arrived in the Green Zone again. We were gathered outside a building, waiting to be taken to a luncheon. I was not sure where we were exactly, but there was high security and they would not let us take pictures. As we stood there waiting for the ambassador to arrive, one of the students in the group pointed to a demolished building nearby and said, "That was Qusay's palace."

What was left of the white stone blocks was covered in soot and the side of the building closest to us had collapsed. I recalled the two patched-up bodies of Qusay and Uday on the news after they had been killed by American marines. Their bodies looked like the wax figures at the horror chamber at Madame Tussauds; they were bloated and bruised, but at the same time shiny and unrealistic.

I looked briefly at the building again and wondered why they had left so many buildings in such ruined states within the Green Zone.

I am not sure why she chose me, but I sat hesitantly at the Ambassador's table, listening to the conversation. Zalmay Khalilzad spoke quietly with a somewhat thick accent. He talked freely about his life as a boy in Afghanistan, his education in the United States, and his current position as the US ambassador to Iraq. He was friendly and easy to talk to and touched upon familiar topics like religious discrimination, the turmoil in his native country, and the future of Iraq. They took photographs of us with him, which we never saw, and took us back to the gate of the Green Zone. I think, like the others there, I felt special and maybe even hopeful for a better future.

I look back now and see how much we were (and are) part of a system that has worked for decades developing and preparing our minds for a form of globalization and occupation. As international students, we leave our homes in search of knowledge and development that, according to the West, can only be gained in their universities. We return to our countries after studying abroad, used to Western lifestyles, and carrying their ideologies and teachings that we incorporate into our own teachings back home. We return with an education, but it is an education that erases our trust in our native systems and lifestyles. We begin to believe that our own people and their traditions and education are backward and limited. We forget our own history; we forget that so much of science and art was established in our Eastern civilizations by our ancestors.

April 2006

As soon as my acceptance letter came, my husband gave his notice of resignation at his workplace and we began to prepare for our departure. We told no one of our decision, except my parents and my father-in-law.

I prepared the house for our long absence. I rolled up the rugs and moved them with the antiques to one of the upstairs rooms. It was already filled with metal trunks of Esam's primary school notebooks and toys and my father-in-law's old police uniforms. The old black iron bedstead with canopy, which I had wanted to use after we had renovated the house, sat gathering dust against one of the walls, piled with boxes of china sets and silver cutlery. Over the past three years, I had stored my late mother-in-law's hand-embroidered sheets and table covers, wrapped in colorful satin *bukatch*—bundles—in one of the oak wardrobes. I could not take them with me, so I opted for two of her small handkerchiefs. I wanted Esam to have something of hers with him when we left. My wedding gown and the dresses from the marriage ceremonies all fitted into one of the other wardrobes. I looked at them one last time and sighed. I had not had the opportunity to enjoy my gowns. I locked the wardrobe doors.

I never thought we would be away so long. I prayed, as I always do before long journeys, and we locked the kitchen door and bid farewell to our home. I would come back alone one last time to receive my student visa before we left for the United States. That house, filled with our short history and the echoes of our memories, would stay empty and silent for a very long time.

SEVEN

Manhattan, Kansas, September 2006

I move in and out of nightmares fed by memories of a life I have left behind only physically. The first night of the invasion repeats itself over and over again, but each time there are different people in my home, the missiles are closer and their screams more terrible. Buried in rubble that chokes and blinds me, I claw my way through charred bodies to get to the surface.

I wake up drenched in sweat, overcome by fear, listening to the loud banging on our apartment door. The first feeling I have is that American troops are outside, breaking down the door of our home in Baghdad. I am back there in our bedroom, the power is out, and I can hear my heart pounding against my chest. I shake Esam awake, plead with him.

"Alamreekan, Alamreekan!" The Americans, the Americans. I keep repeating this, shaking his shoulder.

He wakes up, saying, "Lamees, we are in America."

I am not sure if I am relieved or still terrified. I'm dislocated, lost in the fog of a dream. Finally, I let out a breath, a sigh. But still no relief.

We arrived in Manhattan, Kansas in the middle of a hot and humid summer. I was supposed to be ready for this step in my life. I had lived with my parents in the US and Canada before, I was bilingual and easily spoke English, and I had just left behind a chaotic dysfunctional country where my life and that of my family were under constant threat. But I was far from ready. I had fears, which I had brought with me, along with the excitement and the anticipation of a new kind of life. I also had conflicted feelings as I landed in a country that had been an important part of my childhood, but also the reason behind my need to escape Iraq. I never thought that I would instantly regret going to the United States.

Coming from a vibrant, massive, and historic capital city, Manhattan was a small, featureless town. The hotel where we stayed initially was located far from the mall or supermarkets, except for a Kmart. What was more shocking was the absence of buses and public transport. Esam would compare this city with the images of American cities he had gathered from television and films and was disappointed.

I spent the first three days calling my parents and complaining about my loneliness and isolation. Finally, my father gave up trying to convince me to be patient and said, "If you feel this way, just come back. You cannot live like this."

I knew I had no choice but to stay. We had nowhere to go at this point.

———

I had been warned by my Fulbright contact that I would lose my scholarship if I did not attend the orientation in Tucson. But I postponed my trip to Arizona as much as possible to ensure that we had at least found a place to stay before my departure. So I set aside my homesickness and we began to search in earnest. We went through newspaper classifieds looking for apartments. We noticed that when my husband called with his strong accent to make an inquiry, he would be told immediately that there were no vacancies; on the other hand, whenever I called, I would be invited for a viewing probably because of my American accent. We decided to go out on foot to find a place. But even then, we met managers who pursed their lips upon seeing us and denied that they had vacancies. A couple of times, at the point of signing a contract, they would come up with some excuse to withdraw.

After one of our treks around the neighborhoods close to the university, we decided to call a taxi to take us back to the motel. After a very long wait, during which we sat on the curb outside a convenience store, our taxi finally arrived. As I lifted my son into the van and told him in Arabic to sit down, the driver quickly turned and said, "Are you Iraqi?"

We said yes and he proceeded to laugh. "I am Iraqi too!" he exclaimed in Arabic.

He explained that he owned a taxi business and the driver who was supposed to pick us up was delayed, so he took the call himself. I sat in the back seat and quietly cried with gratitude. I could not believe that we had finally found someone we could talk to. We had never before been so far from family and friends, so cut off from everything that was familiar.

Abu Marwa, our new Iraqi friend, immediately took us to meet his wife, and they invited us for a barbecue that evening in one of the parks close to their home. Their warmth and support made us feel safe and prepared us for the steps ahead. They helped us rent an apartment, buy a car, and furnish our home from garage sales.

Tucson, Arizona 2006

The first night I slept in the dorm room at the University of Arizona, I pushed the dresser and the desk against the door. I do not believe I slept at all. In Iraq, I never had the opportunity to experience living on my own. When I got married at the age of twenty-six, I moved from my father's home to my husband's. Now during my two weeks' orientation in Tucson, Arizona, I had my first actual taste of independence. I missed Esam and Ameen, but I got immersed in my courses and enjoyed the sense of community among the students. People from fifty-one nations had been chosen and I was one of them. We ate together, went grocery shopping in groups, and enjoyed telling each other about our homelands. My schedule kept me busy and I found that I had a desire to go back to studying and learning. When I completed my MA degree in Baghdad in 2001, I almost immediately got married and was with child within two months. Now, after four years of being away from work and study, I felt alive again.

I went back to my new home in Manhattan more confident and ready for the upcoming challenges. Esam had been eager for my return; two weeks with our three-year-old in a new country and very limited English had kept him busy and frustrated. He had bought a television and a mattress and they were using a cardboard box as a dining table. For the duration of my absence, he had cooked the only thing he knew: baked chicken and white rice.

———

During my exit interview for the Department of English at Kansas State in 2008, I was asked about my experience there and I replied, "These were the best two years of my life."

The professor who interviewed me laughed and said something like, "I've heard a lot of good things about this department, but I have never heard that!"

He was not one of the professors who had taught me. He did not know about my past or my experiences in Iraq. He did not understand that during those two years my small family had found peace, gained a new perspective on life, and begun to heal slowly with the help of the teachers and friends that we met there. They had supported me and helped me adjust to my new life in Manhattan and worked with me as I learned how to return to studying and research. Their presence had allowed me to push away the memories of the horrors that I had experienced and to enjoy living in peace. Little by little, I was able to rebuild much of what I had lost during the last few years in Iraq.

Still, we could not avoid the contradictions in our feelings as Iraqis in a Midwestern American town. I had brought with me all the grief and anger that the invasion had caused me to feel; and I struggled with these feelings whenever the topic of Iraq came up. At the same time, I longed to forget that past and find a way to fit into a new life. I realized that I was dealing with PTSD and survivor's guilt. My fear would be triggered by the simplest things.

Lying in the path of frequent tornadoes, Manhattan had sirens in place to warn its citizens. These sirens would sound during monthly warning drills. The first few times when I heard them, I would instinctively put my arms over my head, feel the heat rise up my body and sweat dampen my shirt. Quickly I would realize that there was no missile attack and straighten myself, smile weakly at the students around the room, and try to avoid their curious looks.

I had chosen to concentrate on ethnic American literatures, in particular African American and Native American. But I had to excuse myself from class whenever we discussed battles, beatings, or any form of brutality. Sometimes, while driving alone, running errands, or going to pick Ameen up from daycare, I would begin to sob uncontrollably. Triggers, like the songs "Nasam Alayna al-Hawa" by Fairouz, or "Mihajer" by Hatem al-Iraqi, broke me down, and news from Iraq left me in depression for days. Often I would keep up the appearance of contentment and try to convince myself that I was strong and those moments from my past were gone.

———

One day I showed my supervisor a poem that I had written; it was the first one I wrote after leaving Iraq. I had woken up from a dream at four in the morning and quickly wrote what came to my mind, my return to Baghdad from Al-Suwayrah after the invasion. It was the first draft of "Smoke." My supervisor suggested that I join the creative writing course in the department to help me develop my work. In that course I began to unravel all the trauma that I had carried within me. I wrote about everything that we had endured, about family members and friends we had lost, about a culture that was destroyed by a senseless and unjustified invasion.

I sat in the offices of my instructors and with the little group of friends I had made, as my stories poured out about the people I had left behind, about my incurable homesickness, and my longing for an image of Iraq before the invasion. They calmly listened and sometimes held me, moved to tears themselves.

Not everyone was so kind. Some students still saw me as the enemy; they felt I had no right to be there in their classrooms. In my poetry class, they would question my choice of topics and they were defensive when I spoke about the destruction during the invasion or the emergence of the violence in the aftermath. At times, their ignorance baffled me. In one of my American Literature courses we discussed our thoughts on what America meant to us. I hesitated in my answer, but finally I said, "I am not sure. I haven't been here for very long. I come from a country with six thousand years of history, I don't know what to say about one that is only two-hundred years old."

That evening, my fellow students replied to my comments on the online discussion board with statements like: "Even though we are two hundred years old, we are the most powerful country in the world."

I became anxious and went to the course instructor the following day. I told her that I feared I had offended my classmates, though actually I feared being further attacked by them. I could not understand why they were so aggressive. She told me to ignore their comments and say what I believed. I faced similar comments and attacks in other courses as well, even when the topics had nothing to do with

Iraq. Most of the Americans around me knew nothing about the country their government and their army had destroyed over a period of fifteen years and they did not care.

Manhattan, Kansas 2006

In the Walmart parking lot
My three-year-old begins to step out of the car,
his small tanned face drained of color,
looking horrified.
I follow his gaze,
the car next to us has a soldier's helmet in the back.
"Mama, Amreekan," he whispers.
He seems paralyzed in that spot,
bent forward,
crouching on the back seat,
his eyes glued to the helmet.
I feel like crying, but I laugh instead.
"Habibi, they are all Amreekan."
I pull him out of the car and hold his hand.
His small hand gives me comfort.

Manhattan, Kansas is close to Fort Riley.
We see American soldiers in the stores,
in neighboring houses.
I sit in classrooms with their wives.
I have to suppress a scream
every time one tells me
her husband, boyfriend, friend,
is, was, will be
deployed in Iraq.
An expression spreads
across my face, one

I have not used before.
One that hides
images
of their men in my streets,
dragging our men
by their collars, by their feet, by their hair.

I have to be civil.

Facing a Monster

I say "facing," but actually we were sitting in one of the top rows of Bramlage Coliseum among a crowd of students listening to Donald Rumsfeld. I am not sure why we went, but we sat there trying to control ourselves from crying out. I felt nauseous just looking at him, revulsion rising in the pit of my stomach every time the audience cheered and clapped for him. I feared we were being watched by the crowd around us; and my instinct to run slowly began to amplify with the questions that the audience began to ask. My husband's face had lost color.

He finally turned to me and said, "Let's leave." I nodded.

As soon as we exited through the heavy double doors, I released all the air that was caught in my lungs. My eyes adjusted to the winter light outside and I welcomed the fresh air. We sat in our car, silently staring ahead before we drove out of the parking lot. I am not sure what we had thought we would gain from that experience; it did not change what we felt toward the American invasion nor did it provide a logical explanation for their attack. Somewhere in the back of my mind I think I had hoped that he would show remorse for leading an unwarranted attack that led to so many deaths, including those of his own countrymen so far from their homes.

After we arrived in the States, I received a call from my cousin Hiba. We had been very close before I left Iraq and she was like a sister to me. She got married a few months before I did and our children were born a few months apart. Her first child, Jaffar, was born with Down Syndrome; he had leukemia and multiple health issues that kept his parents struggling with hospitals and lab tests in that difficult aftermath. To my surprise, she was calling from Sweden. I asked her when and how she left Iraq.

"It's only me and Jaffar. Ahmed couldn't come at this time," she said.

"Why?" I inquired.

"I left illegally, with smugglers," she answered quietly.

I paused for a second, then asked, "How did you do that?"

We had heard about smugglers, who arranged for people to leave the country and reach Europe. We knew that these people and the routes they used were highly dangerous, especially for a woman on her own. As we cried over the phone, she shared her story.

"The situation became unbearable," she said. She had feared for her son's life.

Insurgents began kidnapping children with disabilities and tying them with explosives to use them in their attacks.

Additionally, civilian killings were no longer random; they had become more categorized; she said that each week a specific group became targets: one week it was physicians, the next it was lawyers, then it was sanitary workers. They had no idea who was committing those crimes. Her husband, Ahmed, was a physician; and she had a degree in computer science and worked in information technology at a well-known bank. They were constantly afraid they would become targets.

Hiba and Ahmed were Shia, but they lived in a predominately Sunni neighborhood. One day, their neighbor came to inform them that Ahmed's name had come up on a list at the local mosque; he had become a target. Hiba quickly collected a small bag of clothes for them and the neighbor took them to my parents' home in Al-Harthia, which was empty at the time. She thought they would only stay there a few days, but they lived in my parents' home for six months until they left Iraq.

In a single week her coworker at the bank where she worked was killed and two of Ahmed's friends and fellow physicians at the hospital were kidnapped. Then, while walking in Al-Harthia, Ahmed found the body of another one of his friends lying in the street. They could not wait any longer.

"No one wants to leave their country. We had good jobs and I was close to my parents, but we could not take it anymore," she recalled.

They decided that she would leave the country with Jaffar and head toward Sweden. They had enough money to pay for only two of them, so one of them had to stay behind. They paid thirty thousand American dollars, a sum that was difficult to come by even with the jobs that she and Ahmed had held. So she sold anything she could, including her gold jewelry and their furniture. Still, she came up short by ten thousand dollars. She got it from her father.

She was told to dress like a tourist and take no identifying documentation with her on the journey. My cousin is an only child to loving, protective parents. Her decision to leave her parents and her husband would have been a very difficult one to make. However, Jaffar was about four years old and still dealing with health issues that could not be cared for in Iraq at that time. With the country struggling with depleted medical resources and violent conditions, she had no way to help her son receive the attention and care he needed.

Paying the smugglers half the fees, she flew to Turkey with them and some others, taking with her only a backpack and a stroller. She was taken from place to place with no knowledge of where she was going, but was afraid to ask. Part way in the journey, the smugglers demanded the rest of their fees.

"But you asked us to come without any money," she told them. "I am not carrying anything with me now. You will receive the rest of your fees when we get to our destination."

"You will not complete the journey if we are not paid now," they replied. They also threatened other people in her group, telling one man they would harvest his organs to get their money. Hiba immediately reached Ahmed and he quickly sent her the money. By the time she arrived in Stockholm, she was exhausted and traumatized by what she had witnessed along the way. She told the immigration officers that she had no documents and she wanted to apply for asylum because in Baghdad her son's life was in danger. A year later, Ahmed joined them. She went on to complete a master's degree in health informatics and Ahmed completed his specialization in anesthesiology.

We spoke recently over the phone recalling her journey. "How was Jaffar during that ordeal?" I asked.

"Habibi—my darling—he was my light in those dark days. Every time I broke down, he would hug me and put my head on his lap. He kept me sane," she replied.

Even as she spoke, I could hear her heavy, labored breathing; she still struggled with the scars of that traumatic journey.

Finding My Voice

When I began research for my master's thesis, I learned about Arab American writers. As an English major in Iraq, most of the literature I had studied was written by white, British men. I had already read works like *Food for Our Grandmothers* by Joanna Kadi and Etel Adnan's *In the Heart of the Heart of Another Country*. I felt a connection to their writings; in them I saw my own experiences and my own history and culture. I decided that I would work on Arab American women writers. One day, browsing through the shelves at Hale Library, I pulled out a book whose cover showed an image of two women in Iraqi-style abayas holding hands and walking away from a background of smoke in the distance, under the title *The War Works Hard* by Dunya Mikhail.

I checked it out and read it that night in the flicker of my four-year-old's nightlight, on the floor of his bedroom, while I waited for him to fall asleep. I finished the book in that one sitting, crying through poems about Iraqi women searching for the bones of loved ones in mass graves, waiting for the return of husbands and sons from the front, watching their country destroyed on television screens from thousands of miles away.

With my supervisor's encouragement, I began to write about Iraq and Iraqi women writers, narrators, survivors, and rebels. I began to understand that my connection with my country was much deeper and more complicated than I had thought. In those two years of my scholarship, I dug deeper into the cultural and political history of the country I had left behind so eagerly.

Canada in the Margins

As soon as we arrived in the States, Esam applied for immigration to Canada. In our mind, staying in the United States was never really an option. The image of Canada in the media as a tolerant and liberal country was much more appealing than being in a society that considered us, in one way or another, an enemy. While the people I studied with and learned from were supportive and understanding, we still felt vulnerable.

The paperwork took around fourteen months to complete and on the day we received our immigration documents, we broke down crying with joy on the floor of our bedroom. The thought of returning to Iraq had haunted us for months, especially after we learned that I was pregnant with our second child.

Manhattan, January 2008

I found out I was pregnant in the summer of 2007. We had just returned from a trip to Washington DC, where we had gone to renew our Iraqi passports. I had felt extremely tired the whole time we were away and decided to visit a doctor upon our return. When I found out I was pregnant, I vowed that this pregnancy and delivery would be different from my first one in Baghdad. I wanted to enjoy the full experience without fear, stress, and shouting midwives. I brought home all the information pamphlets and followed all the doctor's orders. I ate healthy and made sure that I enjoyed each stage of the pregnancy.

On January 20, I dropped Esam off at the university; he was scheduled to leave later that day for a conference in Atlanta, Georgia. I headed home to get ready for the baby shower that my friend Julie had organized with some of our other friends and professors. The shower was for me and a Saudi friend who had become pregnant at around the same time. I was immensely happy to be a part of this group. Their support had helped me to adjust and thrive during my stay in Manhattan.

I felt blessed as we enjoyed that lovely day of food, presents, and high emotions. When the shower was over, I packed up my gifts and took my son and my sister Shayma, who had been visiting, home. As I unloaded the car, I felt a shock of pain down my belly and my stomach churned. I concluded that I had had too much to eat and maybe I was also feeling a bit cold. It was January, after all. I took a shower, put my son to bed and checked on my sister, who had a stiff neck from earlier that day. I went straight to bed at around 8:30.

Around midnight I woke up with more pain. It took me a couple of minutes to realize that I might be going into labor. My husband was hours away and I did not want to have the baby without him. The following day I tried to go about my business, enduring the contractions and hoping that they were all false alarms. But after my water broke at the local grocery store, I knew that the baby would wait for no one.

At around 1:30 pm, at Mercy Regional Hospital, my beautiful newborn baby boy, Hamza, was placed on my chest. Esam listened to the birth on his cell phone. Shayma, who had brought a camera to record the birth, laughed through streaming tears. I think that my sister and I both felt that we had accomplished a great feat.

Manhattan, Spring 2008

I spent the next few months writing my master's dissertation and caring for the kids, enjoying the feeling of renewed motherhood. My experience with my newborn was very different from that with Ameen. I went on walks, went shopping with the baby, and appreciated feeling safe. Everything I needed for the baby and myself was abundantly available. Esam was also finishing his research for his master's dissertation, and he would spend his time between his research experiments and home. We were not worried about blackouts, kidnappings, or bombings. We did not fear for our lives.

I completed my dissertation as soon as I could, energized by the expectation of settling down with a bright future. My little one seemed to sense the calmness, his contented look and smiles catching the attention of people as we took our strolls. His big blue-green eyes would light up at the sight of our faces, especially his big brother's. They would spend his waking time together, my eldest chatting away while his baby brother sat cooing and babbling in response.

One day, on a very quiet afternoon, in the blooming spring of Manhattan, Kansas, I found myself especially at peace. A feeling I can only describe as *contentment* flowed through every part of my being, a feeling that I had lost many years ago. Less than two years before, I had locked the doors to my home in Baghdad for the last time and left the country with my young family. I had brought with me bitter memories of the American invasion and the violence that followed.

These feelings had been like particles of dust trapped in the corners of my mind. We were now settled in the comfort of a simple, routine, and peaceful life. I felt overwhelmed with gratitude for everything we had in our lives.

As I sat on the oversized sofa in our small townhouse living room, in that serene moment of contentment, I began to gather those memories of Iraq and those pieces of myself that I had cautiously hidden away. I began to write.

> I have never seen seasons fall
> into each other like this.
> Back home,
> both seasons are covered in dust.
> We taste it on our tongues
> on our way to school,
> sometimes grainy and rough,
> other times powdery and light,
> we brush our clothes
> leave behind handprints and streaks,
> we wait for it to settle before we inhale,
> but it coats the very cavities of our lungs.
> Only when it rains do we feel God.
> The falling drops release the smell of the earth.
> The dust defies the rain and starts to rise,
> then gives up, dissolves
> and falls back into piles of mud once again.

EIGHT

Canada, August 2008

We arrived in Kitchener, Ontario at 11:30 at night. I was tired from traveling and delays, and could barely keep my eyes open as a family friend drove us from the Toronto airport to the motel that we had booked. We had chosen Kitchener in our immigration application because we had friends who had immigrated there a year earlier.

Before leaving the States, we had decided that we would return to Jordan to attend my sister Shayma's wedding and see the family. After landing in Canada we would not be able to leave the country for three years if we wanted to apply for citizenship as soon as possible. I was delighted to be a part of her big day. Due to our single-entry visa for the United States, I had not been able to attend any of her pre-wedding ceremonies or be with the family as they planned for the occasion. The only thing we were able to do together was pick out her wedding dress when she had come to visit us in Manhattan.

Our trip to Amman gave us a bit of an energetic charge for the days ahead. We saw family and friends we had not seen for over two years. The gatherings and feasts allowed us to remember what we had missed and longed for during our time away.

When we arrived in Canada, our friends opened their home to us, sharing their meals and storing our things in the little space they had. They took us out to look for furniture and helped us adjust to life in Kitchener. After four weeks in two different motels, we moved into a two-bedroom apartment on Wilson Avenue, nine floors above our friends' apartment. The building was close to a mall, a supermarket, and a bus terminal. Esam began to look for work immediately and I took care of the kids.

Esam took a course in resumé preparation and intensive job searching, and was given a list of potential companies to apply to. He applied to one in Elmira and was soon contacted for an interview. We were immensely excited, because we knew about the current stagnant job market and expected a few months to pass before he found anything. Iraqi families who had arrived before us complained about the difficulty of finding work to match their education; engineers worked at gas stations and in factory lines or could get only temporary retail positions for the holidays. Even trained physicians were struggling with language proficiency exams, and tried to find placements wherever they could in Canada; most ended up in rural or remote areas for the first few years after landing and they complained of the isolation and the cold weather.

Esam's interview went well and he was given the job in Elmira. He looks back fondly at how he proved himself, arriving as a foreigner with no experience in the middle of rural Ontario. He now describes his coworkers like family members and close friends, and he enjoys the sense of belonging he has gained among them.

We began to understand that there was a social divide in the immigrant Iraqi communities that had not existed back home or in the States. Those who had left Iraq to work in the Arab Gulf countries or in Jordan before immigrating to Canada found it much easier to adjust, because they had worked in Western companies, sent their children to private English-medium schools, and saved sufficient money. Some of them, shortly after arriving in Canada, would have one of their family members return to the Gulf for work. The families then lived comfortably and stayed connected to other family members overseas. The other group of Iraqis arrived mostly as refugees from camps in countries like Turkey and Syria; they struggled with language, adjustment, and jobs. While the first group shed many of our traditions, this group held on tightly.

During our two years in America, Esam and I had been busy working for our degrees while trying to find some peace after the havoc we had experienced in Iraq; therefore we were unaware of the changes that had taken place among Iraqis in North America. We found that in Canada the Iraqi community had grown and actively established itself. Iraqis had started social clubs and opened restaurants, founded schools and mosques, and even organized massive concerts where well-known Iraqi entertainers performed. Most of this was actually taking place in Mississauga, where the majority of them had settled.

Kitchener was somewhat far from multicultural when we arrived in 2008. The area had one or two stores that sold Middle Eastern groceries and food, a couple of mosques, though not led by Arab Muslims, and a few Iraqi families. But we were used to being far from any of that; in Manhattan, we had to drive two hours to pick up a bag of pita bread or find halal meat.

Kitchener, Ontario, February 2009

I sit here in the car humming along to "Hey There Delilah" by Plain White T's on the radio. I turn around to check on my younger one, who is half asleep in his car seat. Snowflakes twirl outside my window, collect into mounds and then break free into the air once again. They drift by the houses that, in February, are still adorned with holiday lights and decorations. I stare distantly into another street, far from here, covered with rusty dust where the houses are decorated with the unsettling darkness of soot.

A bell rings, disrupting my vision, pulling me out of my daydream. I try to shake off the dust and soot of the past from my head, look out into the blinding whiteness of the sun reflected in the snow. Before I completely arrive in the present, I hear the giggles of my five-year-old. He's shaping flaky snowballs to throw at my window. I get out of the car, reach down for a clump of snow. He runs, quickly throws a soft, cold ball that shatters into my face and shrieks with delight.

There was a time when all this joy seemed impossible.

I scoop him into my arms.

"Got you! Shlonak?"

"Zain," he answers out of breath.

He has kept a few Arabic words, somewhere in the clutter of his always adapting mind, full of new memories and a very distant sense of home.

"Yala, let's go home."

I buckle his seatbelt, kiss his smooth forehead, breathe in the smell of the sun. I pull out of the parking space; the car swerves slightly on the icy road.

Eventually, spring will come.

Kitchener, Ontario, May 2009

While I was searching for part-time teaching positions at the local universities, I took the opportunity to apply to the PhD program at the University of Waterloo's Department of English Language and Literature. I was hesitant at first and somewhat resistant to the idea of returning to the classroom for another five or six years. However, with encouragement from Esam and my parents, I applied and was accepted.

Before I began the fall semester, we placed our little one in day-care. When he was two, in Baghdad, Ameen had experienced daycare in sporadic "visits" that usually ended with me anxious and frustrated with the endless checkpoints and traffic jams. I even registered him in a daycare in Amman that accepted monthly payments, so he was able to enjoy playing with other children and learning. He loved it and waited for the bus eagerly every morning on my parents' patio. Even in the States, he quickly learned how to get along with his teachers and peers.

Hamza was eighteen months old when he began daycare. I enjoyed being with him; he was calm and easy to care for. Some days he would follow me around the apartment crawling or stumbling around as I finished housework and cooked. Sometimes I would notice a sudden silence and turn around to find that he had fallen asleep on the living room floor. Now it seemed that I was giving away his right to be with me at such an age and my right to enjoy these years with him that I would never experience again.

In the first few weeks, I would hand him to the daycare worker, run away quickly from his outreaching arms and high-pitched squeals, and sit crying in my car for a few minutes. These were the days when I missed living close to my mother. I kept lamenting our isolation; if we were home he would have been with his grandmother, rather than with strangers.

Back to the Classroom

My experience at the University of Waterloo was very different from that at Kansas State. Here I felt isolated and distanced from students and professors; as an older student and a mother of two my only connection to those around me was in the classroom. As soon as I finished the class sessions, I would head either home or to the library to study; the evenings were a struggle between making dinner, putting the kids to bed, and trying to find time to read and complete the assignments. Other students would arrange to meet after class at a local pub or at the Grad House on campus, but for me this was impossible. As I walked between classes, the quiet, poorly lit hallways of Hagey Hall seemed unwelcoming. As the year progressed, I made a couple of friends who were in the MA program, and I did connect with some professors, but I still felt a sense of alienation.

After a course in life writing, I wanted to expand my research on Iraqi women writers and their representations of trauma and displacement. Once again, I delved into stories of war. Some of the works revived memories of the invasion and its aftermath that I thought I had overcome. One text in particular described the torture that occurred in the prisons during Saddam Hussein's reign, and the names of our family acquaintances began to surface. These were people who had disappeared; we had had no knowledge of what happened to them. The work described in agonizing detail the brutality of Iraqi intelligence and the deranged mentality of some of Iraq's most powerful men.

I began to have a nightmare that tormented me repeatedly for several nights. In it I was a prisoner. Disgraced and ashamed, I was standing behind the prison gates, my face swollen from beatings, my head coarsely shaved, waiting for my father to come and get me. A shaved head was a sign of degradation and dishonor; and I was struck with grief and shame that he would see me in such a pitiful condition. I then chose to stay inside the prison. Each time I had that dream, I would wake up with my heart beating fast, tears streaming down my face.

The struggles with my research only increased as I delved further into the traumatic experiences that these women related. There was no one in the department or at home capable of helping me. Esam tried to understand what I was dealing with and encouraged me to step away from the work for a period of time. He had let go of the past and was looking toward the future; he had, over time, cut his connections to Iraq and our experiences there. He was no longer willing to listen to debates on the condition of the country, nor did he listen to the news. According to him, I was unnecessarily bringing back those stressful memories.

I decided to seek counseling, a service provided by the university, but I was faced with another problem: they had no idea how to deal with my condition. The counselor's office was small, comfortable, and tidy, with a soft love seat for his clients. He smiled politely and asked me what troubled me. I began with what was probably the most popular topic among graduate students of my age: stress, fear of failing, and the strain of juggling a young family with schoolwork. He quickly eased my fears and said that what I was going through was normal.

"But I am going through other things that have to do with my past," I said. I told him about my experiences in Iraq and my overwhelming sense of homesickness. He stopped smiling, set down his large mug of coffee and sat up straight in his chair. I don't think he knew what to say. I cannot remember if he actually said anything helpful. I tried to explain the difficulty of reading about the war and putting together my research; he suggested that I abandon the topic and look for something that was not upsetting.

"But people here need to know these stories. No one here understands them, and my work could shed light on them," I insisted. He did not seem to understand this, and he did not provide me with any more advice.

During my second visit, I was emotional and inconsolable. He was shocked and firmly told me to stop crying. I was so surprised by this reaction and the disgusted look on his face that I promptly wiped away my tears and changed the subject. I began to talk about anything outside of what I was really experiencing, until finally he decided to hand me over to a different counselor. I quit going. Whatever I was dealing with, I had to face it on my own.

The Sixth Floor of Dana Porter Library

I stand among the high, packed shelves at DP. Frozen.

My eyes scan for the word *Iraq*.
It's hard to breathe in here.

My native country's name scattered
on the spines of books.
I feel lonely and lost.
Afraid to pull out a book
lest it say something
describe something
that I know I don't want to
I can't
read.

The books stare back at me
waiting.
I can hear them breathe.

Which one?
Which one seems the least threatening?
I don't want a picture of Saddam on the cover.
I fear stories of torture and hate crimes and genocide.
I have read the stories;
I have heard the stories;
I have lived the stories.
I have learned to store them neatly,

somewhere deep and dark.

Somewhere where
my children cannot find them.

My people have become statistics,

numbers listing carnage,
kidnappings,
displacement.
Lumped together
like the charred bodies
in Al-Amiriyah shelter,
stuck together,
molded into one and
clinging by their skin to walls.

One identity.

The pages don't describe
my cousin Hiba's laughter
as we sit in blackouts
on her parents' rooftop;
the smell of klaycha
baking the night before Eid;
my aunt's soft whispers of dawn prayers;
my family's halahel
sending me off
on my wedding day.

Or the moment we left our home in Zayoona
at dawn, just before the sun came up,
my son sleeping in my lap,
my palm on the glass of the car window,
reaching out to hold Baghdad
one last time.

They don't tell our stories
of waiting at borders,
long hours,
harsh roads and harsher words.

They don't speak
of the uncertainty
and the fear
of the journeys
as we moved from
place to place to place.

Here on the sixth floor of DP,
even among the warmth and comfort of books,
I am anxious and exhausted.

———————

 Lamees Al Athari
September 12, 2013 · Kitchener · 👥

My feelings are bundled up into tiny knots of
anger and frustration. The sorrow has, over the
years, sifted out of my body leaving only these
numb feelings of betrayal. My stories always begin
with the war. I feel that the center of my existence
is there, in that hole made by one of the many
missiles aimed at my people. The hole is dark and
crude, jagged and deep, and within it I always find
fear. The war ended ten years ago, but the ripples
of that missile are always vibrating within me. I
have been told that people have stopped
listening, that no one wants to hear the horror
stories, that people are bored and impatient with
things they are unable to connect with. But how
do we tell our stories? We sit around our living
rooms reminding each other of the painful hours
and lightless days. We remember our loved ones
now long gone. We dig for memories hiding in
grandfather clocks and beneath the ashes of our
burnt out pasts. Our stories are what holds and
binds us to that land to what we lost and will
never, ever regain.

The Other Dimension

A Palestinian Lebanese friend once described an aspect of homesickness, something I had felt numerous times. She said that she was driving down a street in Kitchener and suddenly she felt she was on a street in Beirut. She did not mean that she was reminded of that street back home, but rather that she found herself there.

I have experienced this feeling many times; I now eagerly anticipate it. It's like the body is in two spaces: one here and one there. For a second or two, my mind allows me to visit, my eyes are wide open. For a second, I lose myself and enter autopilot; the sights and sounds of my streets are alive and tangible.

A fleeting sensation, rather than a vision.

April 2014

I sit in front of my Mac flipping through images of the American invasion, looking for the "right ones" for my doctoral defense presentation on Iraqi women and trauma. My finger stops scrolling.

I feel a scream rising from my gut.

A woman dressed in blue, surrounded by American soldiers. Their faces are blurred, but the image is very clear.

She is being raped.

Struggling to escape, she is forever frozen in that moment.

April 29 2014

The years between our arrival and this milestone went quickly and for the first time we feel that we have settled somewhere. In 2009 we bought our first home in Kitchener. I have a black-and-white photograph hanging in our family room of us standing behind a "For Sale" sign, Esam carrying Hamza, and Ameen peeking from behind me with his wide smile. We are immigrants claiming our first plot of land.

We were elated with the concept of settling and re-planting our roots.

By 2014, we were waiting for only one thing: our Canadian citizenship. We had gone through the applications and completed our citizenship exam. We had become used to the routine of life in Kitchener. My doctoral defense was scheduled for April 29 and I was looking forward to getting some time off from deadlines and research.

One day in mid April, I received a Notice to Appear to take the Oath of Citizenship. Even before opening the folded paper, I knew what the date for our citizenship ceremony would be. I let out a screech when I saw that it was the same date as my defense. I had to move my defense. If we postponed our citizenship ceremony, there was no telling what date we would get. After making arrangements with my supervisor, the defense was scheduled for the morning so we could make it to the Citizenship and Immigration Center in downtown Kitchener by 1:30 pm.

My close Iraqi friends and my Syrian friend and colleague attended my defense. Their presence calmed me. They had been a part of my journey. We shared a history of trauma and displacement; we had shared the struggles of adjusting to life in the diaspora; we had shared the gains and losses that come with migration. They had become our second family. After my defense was over, they were tearful and proud. I hugged them and we took photos to commemorate the moment, and then I went off with Esam for our second major achievement of the day.

Esam and I drove quickly toward the CIC on Duke Street, going through the Tim Hortons drive-through for a lunch of bagels and coffee on the way. When we arrived, people were beginning to enter the ceremony hall. The room was lined with rows of chairs and everyone came dressed for the occasion. I could feel the tension and the excitement rising inside me as I waited for the ceremony to begin. I had been so busy the past two weeks that I had not had time to think about the magnitude of the step we were taking.

We sat quietly listening to the citizenship judge speaking. I tried hard to listen, but my mind was fogged with memories of our life so far. I recalled the first time I stood with Ameen at school as they sang "O Canada" on one of my volunteer visits. I was overwhelmed with emotion and eager to become a Canadian and feel that I had a place to belong to. For us, it was not only a passport; it was a new beginning and a feeling of hope after years of fear, alienation, and displacement.

What I did not realize was how hard it would be to actually take the oath. With the happiness of that pivotal moment came the realization that I was discarding a part of myself—that part of my identity that was woven into the wrinkles around my eyes, blended with the color of my skin, and was anchored firmly into my very being. As I recited the oath, I rejoiced and mourned over this new self that materialized as the words floated around us in that room, bouncing off the walls, the chairs, and the red and white flags.

October 2014

While our sense of accomplishment was at its highest during that year, we were also struggling to cope with a grave loss. My father-in-law, Ammo Atta, had been diagnosed with pancreatic cancer in February and my husband had been traveling back and forth, trying to help as much as he could. Esam's family had moved to Jordan in 2007 due to the rise of violence in Baghdad.

After attending my convocation, I took my sons to Jordan to visit my father-in-law while he was still able to enjoy their company. I wanted them to remember him as strong and talkative. We stayed in Amman for a month and they had the opportunity to sit with their grandfather and listen to stories about his childhood; they sat at his feet and tried their best to comfort him. I watched the concern in Ameen's eyes as he listened to his grandfather or helped him adjust to a more comfortable position. He seemed to understand that this would be the last time he would see him.

Ammo Atta passed away in October, surpassing the doctor's predictions, but still too soon for us to accept. We mourned his death from our home in Kitchener. My husband had returned the week before, expecting to go back to Jordan once more. He was inconsolable in his grief.

Ammo Atta was buried in Jordan, far from his home, far from his land and his clan, without the presence of all of his sons to comfort him as he closed his eyes one last time.

March 2015

I can follow news of family and friends only on Facebook. The images and comments on my wall are disturbing. A new form of invasion took over our country under the black banner of religion. My Facebook wall is filled with the images and stories of Daesh (ISIL) victims. Like a plague they move into the towns and cities, killing and destroying, leaving nothing behind. Blinded by ignorance and greed, the mayor of Mosul handed over the keys of the city to ISIL fighters, then watched as the terrorists beheaded hundreds of men and raped their women. ISIL's murderous occupation of Iraqi cities and towns drove the country back into chaos. The world watched as families were torn apart, men were executed and women sold like commodities to terrorist fighters.

Everyone has an opinion, but no one has a solution. Like a scab that is scraped again and again, it refuses to heal. We move from dictatorships to occupations to terrorism and self-destruction. How many times can a country fall?

September 2015

About a year after graduation, I was hired by my department as Definite Term Lecturer to teach English academic and creative writing classes. I enjoyed working with students as they developed their ideas and expanded their knowledge, and to be working with people I knew and admired. Esam and I felt that this was all we needed to finally feel at home.

There are days when the students' energy is uplifting and I leave the classroom feeling like I have made a difference. There are days when I feel that twenty-four hours are not nearly enough to teach, raise kids, do research and have a life. There are days when my memories of Iraq sit so heavily on my heart that I cannot even pull myself into the present.

Then I find myself sitting in my office, looking out to the evergreens outside my window, filled with gratitude and wonder at how I arrived here after that long, complicated journey.

I hold tightly to those moments.

Creative Writing

I stand behind the podium as my students write;
they review each other's poetry.
We are in workshop mode.
The sound of pencils
striking the paper
and melamine surfaces of tables,
reminds me

of school days and exams
sitting in crowded classrooms,
in navy blue jumpers,
our white shirts
bleached of dust stains, ironed crisp
our hair up, in tightly bound ponytails,
meticulously held in place with black hairpins

we write what we have memorized by heart,
lines from the hanging poems,
the dense, intricate words
settle right above our heads
in clouds of dust storms,
galloping Arabian mares
and woven goat-hair tents

trickles of sweat
form on the curves
of our barely plucked eyebrows,
the tips of our fingers
grasping painfully on the tips
of slipping pencils,
the pencils quickly tracing
the arcs and lines of expression
down on the white lined paper,

we try to seize all the accents and metaphors
gathered the night before,
try to catch the phrases
between the neighbors'
arguments outside our windows,
try to catch the light
before the kerosene lamps fade
try to hear the thoughts in our heads
before another missile finds its way.

I hear the graphite hit the wood beneath our papers on the
   desks,
we shift uncomfortably on the wooden benches.

August 2016

We decided to buy a larger house to accommodate our growing boys and my family's visits. In reality, I had longed for a larger house ever since I left my own in Baghdad. I wanted something with a proper living room to hold all our friends and enough room for a large dining table that could take all the trays of lamb and eggplant casseroles. So we bought another house, this time close to the Grand River. Maybe I was hoping that the attachment I had with Dijla would be found right here in Canada.

We have gained so much since we arrived in Canada. Unlike the total seven-year isolation from family that my parents endured in the 1980s, we were blessed with the ability to see ours about once a year, maybe twice if we were lucky. We gather ourselves, each of us now from a different continent, and try to rebuild the bonds that have kept us so close over the years. But the distance creates gorges between us as we grow separately from each other. Our approaches to life, traditions, and religion have changed from those we left cradled in the comfort of our families; our new selves have shed many skins along the way. Since we received our citizenship, we have tried to meet once a year, for a couple of weeks, for a family gathering. We seize this time to allow our children to learn about each other, sit together for meals, and enjoy the warmth that belonging and closeness brings. During the other months of the year, we are connected through technology that allows us a good conversation or two a couple of times a week, which is never really enough.

My Father and My Memories

He tells me to write
about anything,
except the invasion.

He looks up toward the statue
of Queen Victoria.
She is telling my story,
in my voice,
in the middle of
a park in Kitchener.
I am one of the seven narrators
in the Queen Victoria Project.

I watch his very serious
and solemn face
as Victoria's lips
explain my fears
of eliminating, executing
my Iraqi self
here in Canada.

The concept of a
hybrid self seems
unrealistic after
all these years.

He walks slowly,
carrying
those years,
in minutes
stacked upon his shoulders.

He doesn't talk to my boys
or me. There is
a purpose in his steps,
as he walks away from us.

He seems afraid of
opening his mouth

spilling out
those moments
he so fervently
wanted us to

forget.

Talk about the days
before the war, he says.
Why do you hold on
to those memories?
he finally asks.

I don't have an answer.

Reactive Racism 2017

At an event at the Grad House on campus, a bearded elderly man, a well-known university professor, is talking with me, chatting about his work as a writer and how students have changed over the years. Without my realizing it, he has moved on to issues that concern me, talking about "those others," referring to the rise in the number of foreigners and immigrants in the region. He loudly proclaims his inability or refusal to understand their cultures, lifestyles, and languages. He is upset that there are so many of "them." He says that he would never visit a foreign country like mine—of course he incorrectly refers to my country as "Iran" not "Iraq," displaying his ignorance.

I was raised to respect elders; they should be excused when rambling on about issues we do not agree on. But at that moment, I feel the need to clamp his mouth tightly shut with my hand. I stop listening for a moment and watch his mouth open and shut like those of the characters in old cartoons, his arms flailing, his eyes bulging, and strands of white hair shooting up from his scalp.

He says, "The other day, I saw a man dressed fully in his traditional dress, I'm not sure if he was from Pakistan—it was some Eastern country—but I wanted to stop the car and ask what he was doing here. I wanted to tell him to go back where he came from!"

I remain silent. I know only a couple of people in that room. I look around, as he continues from one topic to another. I am the only non-white person in the room. My throat feels dry.

I say, "I think I hear my phone, excuse me."

I dial my husband's number and tell him, "Please come now. I don't think I can take it anymore."

I was never raised to hate other human beings based on the color of their skin, their culture, their social class, or even their ideology. I was never raised to hate. But lately, I feel that I have become a little racist myself. I call it "reactive racism," a position that is an escalating reaction to the discrimination that I and my friends experience at times. It is a position that began in Manhattan, Kansas, but it has grown and strengthened in Canada.

The belief that Canadians are more tolerant of foreigners than their neighbors to the south is not true. In my experience, discrimination in Canada has intensified over the past few years. Maybe it is due to the rising number of refugees and immigrants in the country and the images of us in the media. Maybe it was there all the time and we kept ignoring it in the hope that it was simply in our imagination.

The other day, I was invited to a gathering of Iraqi women. As we sat around the table sipping tea with a spread of taboula, kabab, and kubba, our conversations drifted toward our experiences with "white Canadians," or, as we emphasize, "Canadian Canadians," to distinguish them from nonwhite Canadians.

My hosts, all working women, disclosed the most absurd stories about their day-to-day encounters with white Canadians. There were stories about the occasional rude drivers, but others were much more disturbing.

"As soon as they see the color of our skin, something changes in their attitude," one said.

"It's the hijab," another answered back.

She recounted an experience.

"I was leaving the store, when I accidently bumped the side of a parked car with my leather handbag. The owner of the car leaped out and yelled at me."

The car was neither scratched nor damaged in any way, but the owner kept yelling at her. So the Iraqi woman apologized and suggested calling her insurance company, and she asked the car owner (a woman) what else she would like her to do.

The owner replied, "Apologize."

So she apologized, again. The Iraqi woman asked if she wanted anything else because she needed to get on with her day.

The owner replied, "Apologize again."

Hearing this, we uttered every kind of expletive, in Arabic and English, and cursed the driver, her father, and her father's father.

"What did you do next?" I asked.

"I turned around and left," she said.

We recalled our sense of pride and belonging back home and the humiliations we had suffered at one time or another since leaving Iraq.

On January 29 2017 an armed man entered the mosque of the Islamic Cultural Centre in Quebec City and opened fire on the congregation that had just completed their prayers. The news was shocking to Canadians, who for a long time had not witnessed such acts of terrorism. I attended the rally that my colleagues at the university had organized to denounce the hate crime. I could not speak or share my feelings, but I stood listening to the speeches in that biting cold day with my friend Ashley by my side. She had a cold and I could tell that she needed to be indoors to rest and stay warm. I was grateful for her presence and her support, and I felt angry and sorrowful for the victims and their families. Like them, we had moved here to protect our children from the violence back home. Where could we go from here?

Then, on March 15 2019 an armed man took the lives of worshipers at Christchurch Mosque in New Zealand during Friday prayers. The terrorist act in such a peaceful country shocked the global community. I decided that I would never take my children to large Muslim gatherings.

But the acts did not push me away from my beliefs; instead I began feeling the need to return to my religious practices, and this past Ramadan was the first time in a very long time that I was able to fast most of the month and complete reading the Quran.

Muslima

Lately,
I question everything.
I watch as they struggle to contain themselves
on the screen.
Their voices seem to spill into our living room
the miles and oceans compressed between us.

Bent forward, body yielding
forehead pressed
against the thinly threaded mat, I try
to catch
the verses fluttering
in the creases of my brain.

They have retreated deeper and deeper beyond
the reach of my fingertips. Pushed away
by frigid Ontario winters
and the fear of being the Other.

Other in my language, in my skin
in my thoughts, in my prayers.

Other than my neighbor or my colleague or the man walking
his dog down the street.
I hide behind my perfected American accent, my tight jeans
and my unveiled head.

My body bends, this time in resistance,
verses form
I can taste them,
feel them coil around
my tongue and declare their existence

The Canada Effect

I complain about my life away from home and my incurable homesickness, and the instances of discrimination I have experienced, but I
know that our lives here in Canada have been the best they can be. We
are blessed with belonging to a nation that has accepted us, supported
us, and allowed us to grow. We are also blessed with our memories of
the past, so that we are able to compare the life we left behind with
the place we have now called home. Our memories are the warmth we
reach for on those cold nights, under our heavy duvets as the house
moans under the impact of the wailing winds outside.

We keep them close, these memories, reaching out to them whenever we feel lost.

Ameen sometimes asks if I ever think about our lives had we stayed
in Baghdad. I tell him that the thought is often on my mind. I do not
tell him that my heart stops when I think about him leaving the house
to venture outside into Baghdad's streets. We left to keep him safe, to
give him, and now his brother, the opportunity to live and dream and
thrive. That is what we have gained. I enjoy Hamza's playful attempts

at trying to pronounce words in Arabic and his interest in hearing my stories about growing up in Iraq. Although he has never been to Iraq, he seems connected to it through these stories.

I sometimes tell them that they are spoiled here, they cannot even imagine what boys their age endure back home, but I think we have all been spoiled and blessed. Our minds have opened to new possibilities and ideals that have taken us farther away from home than any physical distance can ever do. We have made friends from every corner of the world—people we would never have met in Iraq. We have become part of the fabric here.

June 2018

Talking with my mother on the phone, our conversation veered toward Al-Harmia. My parents had settled in Amman, Jordan, but they had stayed very connected with family members back home. She was complaining because the Iraqi government had prohibited landowners and farmers to grow crops in the upcoming year due to water shortages. Turkey has built the Ilisu Dam on the Tigris, which will critically impact Iraq's water supply. We went through this crisis before. In the early 1970s my father's family was forced to leave their home and move to Baghdad due to a drought. My mom used to tell us how they thought she was a good omen because around the time my parents got married in 1976, water flowed once again in the Chehat River—the river near my grandfather's home. In the first Gulf War, I recall that the river dried up again. We were left with green bacteria-rich puddles in place of the river.

Over the years, such issues have led to villagers migrating to nearby cities as families look for more sustainable work and living conditions. The demographics of the area will once again change or, maybe this time, disappear altogether.

May 2019

A couple of weeks ago, I asked my father to send me some pictures of our village, Al-Harmia, to add to my memoir. He sent me the picture below of the Abu Skhair River that runs through a nearby town with the same name. I was surprised by the lush green vegetation and the high waters of the river. I called him and inquired about the drought.

"Baba, I thought that we were going through a drought. Mama said they were expecting the river to dry up and that farmers were forbidden from planting crops."

"Yes, that was the case," Baba replied, "but Allah is gracious. This year we had so much rain, the rivers are full and we were able to plant rice again."

My eyes teared up with hope.

"Alhamdullah," I replied, "inshallah it's like this every year."

After the Rain

The rain in my county is a gift from heaven.
Long awaited,
it cleanses the leaves and flowers,
the streets and buildings,
and more importantly, our lives.
In the few hours when it stops,
our life has hope
and we dare to dream.
The rain seeps through the cracks,
fills the potholes in the streets, and overflows onto the sidewalks.
The air is filled with the raw smell of the earth
as she dances, embracing raindrops as they fall.
The palm trees sway,
we sway to the sounds of raindrops
striking stone driveways and shanasheel,
drenching rice fields and dirt roads.

In my country, the rain falls like a celebration.

AFTERWORD

————

A couple of years ago, I sat sipping coffee in a little Toronto cafe with Nurjehan Aziz, the publisher at Mawenzi House. As we chatted about my work and exchanged stories about our cultural backgrounds, I felt that my story would be in safe hands. I am grateful that she accepted my book, when it was somewhere between a nine-page concept and a memoir. I thank them for their time, patience and commitment.

As I dived into memories of home and the events that led me to leave, I found that these memories and reflections were rather complex. Through this memoir, I tried to present my own perspective of life as an Iraqi woman. By no means does this work represent all Iraqi women, nor does it aim to cover all Iraqi experiences of the American invasion and the aftermath that followed. My family and I have been blessed to have survived the violence and displacement that so many Iraqis endured.

I am also blessed to have people in my life that provide me with opportunities to grow and support me unconditionally. First and foremost, I am grateful to my husband, Esam, who spent hours reading my work, discussing the stories, and holding me together as I struggled with some of the more overwhelming memories.

My boys, Ameen and Hamza, have been the motivation for

completing this work. Since I left Iraq, I have tried to pass on to them pieces of our culture and fragments of my memories so they can connect to their roots and their histories.

My deepest love and gratitude to my parents, whose love for Iraq has instilled in me unrelenting pride in my homeland and its generous people. Many thanks to my brother and sister, Haydar and Shayma, and my sister-in-law, Sara, who have been my best friends for as long as I can remember. Special thanks to my father and Haydar for the images they sent me of Al-Harmia and the neighboring areas, which reveal the beauty of this rarely explored place in the world.

So many of my loved ones allowed me to share their stories and include their names in this work. My aunts, uncles, in-laws and cousins have all been an essential part of my life and I thank them for allowing me to include them in my work. Especially, I would like to thank my cousin Hiba for graciously sharing her story with me.

I would like to thank Barbara Aziz for all the conversations we shared about Iraq and for the documents she generously gave me; they added so much to my own knowledge of the impacts of war and sanctions on the Iraqi people.

Many thanks to *The New Quarterly* editors, Pamela Mulloy and Susan Scott, for offering me countless hours of their time and support throughout the writing process.

I am grateful for my friends and colleagues, Ashley Mehlenbacher and Andrea Jonahs, for their friendship and encouragement over the past few years.

Last, but definitely not least, much gratitude and love to my Iraqi and Arab friends for their tremendous support and their kindness in sharing their stories.